Map Key

Trail Name	Page
PART 1 SOUTH	
OREGON BORDER TO WHITE PASS	
1 Gillette Lake [*Day hike, Out-and-back, 5 miles*]	24
2 Bunker Hill [*Day hike, Out-and-back, 3.6 miles*]	29
3 Lemei Lake [*Day hike/1 night, Semiloop, 12.5 miles*]	34
4 Horseshoe Meadow [*Day hike/ 1 night, Out-and-back, 10 miles*]	41
5 Nannie Ridge [*Day hike/ 1 night, Loop, 14.5 miles*]	46
6 Old Snowy Mountain [*2–3 days, Out-and-back, 26 miles*]	51
7 Round Mountain [*Day hike, Out-and-back, 12 miles*]	58
PART 2 CENTRAL	
WHITE PASS TO STEVENS PASS	
8 Buesch and Dumbbell Lakes [*Day hike/1 night, Loop, 16 miles*]	66
9 Laughingwater Creek [*Day hike/1 night, Out-and-back, 12–20 miles*]	73
10 Dewey Lake [*Day hike, Loop, 8 miles*]	79
11 Sheep Lake and Sourdough Gap [*Day hike, Out-and-back, 6.4 miles*]	84
12 Bullion Basin to Silver Creek [*Day hike, Loop, 7 miles*]	89
13 Big Crow Basin [*Day hike/1 night, Loop, 12.5 miles*]	95
14 Mirror Lake [*Day hike, Loop, 6 miles*]	101
15 Commonwealth Basin to Red Pass [*Day hike, Out-and-back, 10 miles*]	107

Trail Name	Page
16 Spectacle Lake [*2–3 days, Out-and-back, 20 miles*]	112
17 Cathedral and Deception Passes [*Day hike/1 night, Loop, 14.5 miles*]	118
18 Surprise and Glacier Lakes [*Day hike, Out-and-back, 10 miles*]	125
19 Hope and Mig Lakes [*Day hike, Out-and-back, 4 miles*]	130
20 Chain and Doelle Lakes [*3–4 days, Out-and-back, 22 miles*]	135
PART 3 NORTH	
STEVENS PASS TO CANADIAN BORDER	
21 Lake Valhalla [*Day hike/1 night, Point-to-point, 8.5 miles*]	144
22 Cady Ridge to Kodak Peak [*2–3 days, Out-and-back, 18 miles*]	149
23 Little Giant Pass [*Day hike, Out-and-back, 10 miles*]	155
24 Buck Creek Pass [*2–3 days, Out-and-back, 19 miles*]	161
25 Lyman Lake and Suiattle Pass [*2-5 days, Out-and-back, 22 miles*]	167
26 Agnes Creek [*3–5 days, Out-and-back, 38 miles*]	173
27 Rainbow Lake and McAlester Creek [*3–5 days, Loop, 31.5 miles*]	180
28 Cutthroat Pass [*Day hike/1 night, Out-and-back, 10 miles*]	188
29 Grasshopper Pass [*Day hike/ 1 night, Out-and-back, 11 miles*]	193
30 Tamarack Peak [*Day hike, Out-and-back, 8–10 miles*]	198

DAY & SECTION HIKES

Pacific Crest Trail
WASHINGTON

ADRIENNE SCHAEFER

WILDERNESS PRESS . . . *on the trail since 1967*

BERKELEY, CA

Day & Section Hikes Pacific Crest Trail: Washington

1st EDITION 2010

Copyright © 2010 by Adrienne Schaefer

Front cover photographs copyright © by John Schaefer (top) and author (bottom)
Interior photographs by author
Maps by Scott McGrew and author
Cover design by Scott McGrew
Book design by Ian Szymkowiak/Palace Press International

ISBN 978-0-89997-509-2

Manufactured in the United States of America

Published by: **Wilderness Press**
1345 8th Street
Berkeley, CA 94710
(800) 443-7227; FAX (510) 558-1696
info@wildernesspress.com
www.wildernesspress.com

Visit our website for a complete listing of our books and for ordering information.
Distributed by Publishers Group West

Cover photos: Lyman Lake (top, Hike 25) and Nannie Ridge (bottom, Hike 5)
Frontispiece: Descending into Plummer Basin (Hike 26)

SAFETY NOTICE: Although Wilderness Press and the author have made every attempt to ensure that the information in this book is accurate at press time, they are not responsible for any loss, damage, injury, or inconvenience that may occur to anyone while using this book. You are responsible for your own safety and health while in the wilderness. The fact that a trail is described in this book does not mean that it will be safe for you. Be aware that trail conditions can change from day to day. Always check local conditions, know your own limitations, and consult a map.

Table of Contents

Overview Map   inside front cover
Map Key   i
Acknowledgments   viii
Preface   x
Recommended Hikes   xii
Introduction   I

PART 1: SOUTH
OREGON BORDER TO WHITE PASS   23

 I Gillette Lake [Day hike, Out-and-back, 5 miles]   24
 2 Bunker Hill [Day hike, Out-and-back, 3.6 miles]   29
 3 Lemei Lake [Day hike/1 night, Semiloop, 12.5 miles]   34
 4 Horseshoe Meadow [Day hike/1 night, Out-and-back, 10 miles]   41
 5 Nannie Ridge [Day hike/1 night, Loop, 14.5 miles]   46
 6 Old Snowy Mountain [2—3 days, Out-and-back, 26 miles]   51
 7 Round Mountain [Day hike, Out-and-back, 12 miles]   58

PART 2: CENTRAL
WHITE PASS TO STEVENS PASS   65

 8 Buesch and Dumbbell Lakes [Day hike/1 night, Loop, 16 miles]   66
 9 Laughingwater Creek [Day hike/1 night, Out-and-back,
    12—20 miles]   73
IO Dewey Lake [Day hike, Loop, 8 miles]   79
II Sheep Lake and Sourdough Gap [Day hike, Out-and-back,
    6.4 miles]   84
I2 Bullion Basin to Silver Creek [Day hike, Loop, 7 miles]   89
I3 Big Crow Basin [Day hike/1 night, Loop, 12.5 miles]   95
I4 Mirror Lake [Day hike, Loop, 6 miles]   IOI

15 Commonwealth Basin to Red Pass [*Day hike, Out-and-back, 10 miles*] 107

16 Spectacle Lake [*2–3 days, Out-and-back, 20 miles*] 112

17 Cathedral and Deception Passes [*Day hike/1 night, Loop, 14.5 miles*] 118

18 Surprise and Glacier Lakes [*Day hike, Out-and-back, 10 miles*] 125

19 Hope and Mig Lakes [*Day hike, Out-and-back, 4 miles*] 130

20 Chain and Doelle Lakes [*3–4 days, Out-and-back, 22 miles*] 135

PART 3: NORTH
STEVENS PASS TO CANADIAN BORDER 143

21 Lake Valhalla [*Day hike/1 night, Point-to-point, 8.5 miles*] 144

22 Cady Ridge to Kodak Peak [*2–3 days, Out-and-back, 18 miles*] 149

23 Little Giant Pass [*Day hike, Out-and-back, 10 miles*] 155

24 Buck Creek Pass [*2–3 days, Out-and-back, 19 miles*] 161

25 Lyman Lake and Suiattle Pass [*2–5 days, Out-and-back, 22 miles*] 167

26 Agnes Creek [*3–5 days, Out-and-back, 38 miles*] 173

27 Rainbow Lake and McAlester Creek [*3–5 days, Loop, 31.5 miles*] 180

28 Cutthroat Pass [*Day hike/1 night, Out-and-back, 10 miles*] 188

29 Grasshopper Pass [*Day hike/1 night, Out-and-back, 11 miles*] 193

30 Tamarack Peak [*Day hike, Out-and-back, 8–10 miles*] 198

Appendix A: Park Contacts 205

Appendix B: Managing Agencies 207

Index 209

About the Author 218

Map Legend inside back cover

For my family—I love you all
and thank you for your support.

Acknowledgments

I WOULD FIRST LIKE TO THANK Amanda and Judy Ford for discovering this opportunity and encouraging me to pursue it. I am forever grateful to both my parents for supporting me through all of my crazy endeavors and owe my mom special thanks for hiking on trails she would have rather read about. I could fill an entire page with things I would like to thank my husband John for, but sticking by my side through the ups and downs of this bumpy adventure is probably the most important.

Tyler and Lindsay Kellet get special recognition for spending a semi-hypothermic afternoon on Little Giant Pass with me, and their words of advice helped make this book what it is. Numerous folks kept me company on the trails, including Aaron Sherred, Mike and Maurisa Descheemaeker, Reggie Descheemaeker, Rebecca Lofgren, Terri and Stacy, Jen Glyzenski, and Carla. Thank you to the crew from Carlton, John Jorgenson, Surya and Bhavesh Dinodica, and Zeke and Kathleen Hirschstein for sharing their amazing garden (are you sure it's organic?) and their homes with me. My good friends at Mount Rainier National Park kept me entertained on rest days, and Rebecca A., Andy, and Barry (you were my saving grace up at Three Lakes) made me feel right at home. While I am a country bumpkin at heart, there's nothing quite like a night of good wine and great food after a day's hike; thanks to Bob and Sarah White for a memorable weekend in Portland. When I couldn't drag anyone out, I could always count on my parent's dog, Maggie, to join me. Come rain or shine, her enthusiasm to be out was contagious. I should also include a few other four-legged friends: Hazel, Cali, Juneau, and Nez.

Thank you to all the men and women who braved the mountains when they were truly wild and laid the foundation for what we have today. My hiking experiences would not have been nearly as enjoyable if not for the hard work of the National Park Service and U.S. Forest Service employees who maintain our roads, trails, and bridges. Researching, writing about, and hiking these trails could not have been done without the help of countless other resources, including Dr. Fred T. Darvill Jr.'s *Hiking the North Cascades,* Ira and Vicky Spring and Harvey Manning's *100 Hikes* series, Chester Marler's *East of the Divide,* and Andy Selters's *Pacific Crest Trail: Oregon and Washington,* also published by Wilderness Press. Their words were truly inspiring.

To all of the other people who touched my life in one way or another during this incredible journey through the Washington Cascades, thank you.

Preface

JUST OUTSIDE MOUNT ST. HELEN'S NATIONAL VOLCANIC MONU-
MENT lies the small town of Cougar, Washington. It is your typical
mountain town, complete with a diner, tavern, convenience store,
and RV park (actually two of them). Normally I would continue down
the road to a more primitive site, but exhaustion prevailed and the
next thing I knew I was driving by the neon flashing vacancy light of
the RV park.

I knocked on the door and was immediately greeted by a friendly
couple. They invited me into their home and I told them I was looking for a tent site. They gave me a quick head to toe, and I suddenly
became aware of how I must look; my legs were covered with a thick
coat of dust, my hair was matted from too many days under a hat, and
my clothes were a wrinkled, dirty mess. The woman spoke first, saying, "Well, it looks like you need to treat yourself to a good night's
sleep." I informed her I was on a budget and she waved her hand,
telling me not to worry. The next thing I knew, I was unlocking the
door to a sweet little cabin with clean towels in hand.

Throughout my time exploring Washington's Pacific Crest Trail
(PCT), spontaneous moments like this were part of what made my
trips so memorable. Whether it was fresh goat cheese from a gardener
in Stehekin, homemade honey from a street vendor in Hood River,
colorful veggies from the Twisp Farmers Market, or a hot cup of
espresso from the hardware store in Plain, each mountain community
surrounding the PCT has something unique to offer.

This book is a culmination of my experiences along a trail full of
culture, history, and breathtaking scenery. Selecting 30 of my favorite hikes was no easy task. Like the communities that surround the
PCT, each trail offers something special that sets it apart from the
others. I found myself on numerous occasions saying, "I had no idea

this place was so beautiful. This hike is definitely going in the book."
Or perhaps it was a bit of history that caught my attention, such as
finding an old sheepherder trail or seeing the remnants of an abandoned fire lookout.

In the end, I whittled them down to 30 spectacular hikes that
stretched from the mighty waters of the Columbia River to the majes-
tic peaks of the North Cascades. The actual task of hiking all the trails
was no easy feat. I would be lying if I said my trip to Chain Lakes in
a torrential downpour was a highlight of my hiking career. But as
time fades, memories of napping on sun-baked rocks, taking a dunk
in alpine lakes, or watching alpenglow dance on snowcapped peaks
replace those less desirable moments.

This book will inspire you to discover a side of Washington you
may have never seen, whether you've lived here your whole life or are
just passing through. Hike with open eyes and your journey through
this beautifully diverse state will bring you as much fulfillment as I
experienced while hiking these trails.

Recommended Hikes

Best Overnight Hikes with Kids

1 Gillette Lake (*page 24*)
11 Sheep Lake and Sourdough Gap (*page 84*)
14 Mirror Lake (*page 101*)
16 Spectacle Lake (*camp at Pete Lake*) (*page 112*)
21 Lake Valhalla (*page 144*)

Best Hikes with Dogs

1 Gillette Lake (*page 24*)
8 Buesch and Dumbbell Lakes (*page 66*)
13 Big Crow Basin (*page 95*)
14 Mirror Lake (*page 101*)
18 Surprise and Glacier Lakes (*page 125*)

Best Hikes for Wildflower Viewing

4 Horseshoe Meadow (*page 41*)
10 Dewey Lake (*page 79*)
13 Big Crow Basin (*page 95*)
23 Little Giant Pass (*page 155*)
24 Buck Creek Pass (*page 161*)

Best Loop Hikes

3 Lemei Lake (*page 34*)
12 Bullion Basin to Silver Creek (*page 89*)
17 Cathedral and Deception Passes (*page 118*)

26 Agnes Creek (*page 173*)
27 Rainbow Lake and McAlester Creek (*page 180*)

Best Hikes for Alpine Vistas

15 Commonwealth Basin to Red Pass (*page 107*)
22 Cady Ridge to Kodak Peak (*page 149*)
23 Little Giant Pass (*page 155*)
28 Cutthroat Pass (*page 188*)
29 Grasshopper Pass (*page 193*)

Hikes with Best Swimming Holes

5 Nannie Ridge (*page 46*)
7 Round Mountain (*page 58*)
8 Buesch and Dumbbell Lakes (*page 66*)
9 Laughingwater Creek (*page 73*)
19 Hope and Mig Lakes (*page 130*)

Best Hikes to Summits

6 Old Snowy Mountain (*page 51*)
7 Round Mountain (*page 58*)
14 Mirror Lake (*page 101*)
22 Cady Ridge to Kodak Peak (*page 149*)
30 Tamarack Peak (*page 198*)

Best Hikes for an Escape (Solitude)

2 Bunker Hill (*page 29*)
3 Lemei Lake (*page 34*)
20 Chain and Doelle Lakes (*page 135*)
23 Little Giant Pass (*page 155*)
26 Agnes Creek (*page 173*)

Most Difficult Hikes

6 Old Snowy Mountain (*page 51*)
16 Spectacle Lake (*page 112*)
22 Cady Ridge to Kodak Peak (*page 149*)
23 Little Giant Pass (*page 155*)
27 Rainbow Lake and McAlester Creek (*page 180*)

Easiest Hikes

1 Gillette Lake (*page 24*)
11 Sheep Lake and Sourdough Gap (*page 84*)
28 Cutthroat Pass (*page 188*)
29 Grasshopper Pass (*page 193*)
30 Tamarack Peak (*page 198*)

Hikes Mostly on the PCT

11 Sheep Lake and Sourdough Gap (*page 84*)
21 Lake Valhalla (*page 144*)
24 Buck Creek Pass (*page 161*)
28 Cutthroat Pass (*page 188*)
29 Grasshopper Pass (*page 193*)

RECOMMENDED HIKES

Dewey Lake (Hike 10)

Introduction

How to Use This Guidebook

The Overview Map and Key

USE THE OVERVIEW MAP on the inside front cover to assess the exact locations of each hike's primary trailhead. Each hike's number appears on the overview map, on the map key facing the overview map, and in the table of contents.

The book is organized into three regions as indicated in the table of contents. The hikes within each region are noted as one-way day hikes, loop day hikes, or overnight loop hikes (see pages v–vi). A map legend that details the symbols found on trail maps appears on the inside back cover.

Trail Maps

Each hike contains a detailed map that shows the trailhead, the route, significant features, facilities, and topographic landmarks, such as creeks, overlooks, and peaks. The author gathered map data by carrying a GPS unit (Garmin eTrex) while hiking. This data was downloaded into a digital mapping program (Topo USA) and processed by expert cartographers to produce the highly accurate maps found in this book. Each trailhead's GPS coordinates are included with each profile (see page 2).

Elevation Profiles

Each hike contains a detailed elevation profile that corresponds directly to the trail map. The elevation profile provides a quick look at the trail from the side, enabling you to visualize how the trail rises and falls. Key points along the way are labeled. Note the number of feet between each tick mark on the vertical axis (the height scale). To avoid making flat hikes look steep and steep hikes appear flat, height scales are used throughout the book to provide an accurate assessment of each hike's climbing difficulty.

GPS TRAILHEAD COORDINATES

To collect accurate map data, each trail was hiked with a handheld GPS unit (Garmin eTrex series). Data collected was then downloaded and plotted onto a digital USGS topo map. In addition to rendering a highly specific trail outline, this book also includes the GPS coordinates for each trailhead in two formats: latitude/longitude and UTM. Latitude/longitude coordinates tell you where you are by locating a point west (latitude) of the 0-degree meridian line that passes through Greenwich, England, and north or south of the 0-degree (longitude) line, the equator, that belts the Earth.

Topographic maps show latitude/longitude as well as UTM grid lines. Known as UTM coordinates, the numbers index a specific point, using a grid method. The survey datum used to arrive at the coordinates in this book is WGS84 (versus NAD27 or WGS83). For readers who own a GPS unit, whether handheld or onboard a vehicle, the latitude/longitude or UTM coordinates provided on the last page of each hike may be entered into the GPS unit. Just make sure your GPS unit is set to navigate using WGS84 datum. Now you can navigate directly to the trailhead.

Most trailheads, which begin in parking areas, can be reached by car, but some trailheads are a short walk from a parking area. In those cases a handheld unit is necessary to continue the GPS navigation process. That said, readers can easily access all trailheads in this book by using the directions given, the overview map, and the trail map, which shows at least one major road leading into the area. But for those who enjoy using the latest GPS technology to navigate, the necessary data has been provided. A brief explanation of the UTM coordinates from Gillette Lake (page 24) follows.

UTM Zone 10T
Easting 0583256
Northing 5055921

The UTM zone number (10) refers to one of the 60 vertical zones of the Universal Transverse Mercator (UTM) projection. Each zone is 6 degrees wide. The UTM zone letter (T) refers to one of the 20 horizontal zones that span from 80 degrees south to 84 degrees north. The easting number (0583256) indicates in meters how far east or west a point is from the central meridian of the zone. Increasing easting coordinates indicate that you are moving east; decreasing easting coordinates indicate that you are moving west. The northing number (5055921) references in meters how far you are from the equator. Above and below the equator, increasing northing coordinates indicate you are traveling north; decreasing northing coordinates indicate you are traveling south. To enhance your outdoor experiences with GPS technology, refer to *Outdoor Navigation with GPS* by Steve Hinch and also published by Wilderness Press.

THE HIKE PROFILE

In addition to a map, each hike contains a concise but informative narrative of the hike from beginning to end. This descriptive text is enhanced with at-a-glance ratings and information, GPS-based trailhead coordinates, and accurate driving directions leading from a major road to a parking area convenient to the trailhead.

At the top of the section for each hike is a box that allows the hiker quick access to pertinent information: quality of scenery, condition of trail, appropriateness for children, difficulty of hike, quality of solitude expected, hike distance, approximate time of hike, and outstanding highlights of the trip.

The first five categories are rated using a five-star system. See the following page for an example. In this example, the two stars indicate that the scenery is somewhat picturesque. The trail condition is good (one star would mean the trail is muddy, rocky, overgrown, or

I Gillette Lake

SCENERY: ✿ ✿
TRAIL CONDITION: ✿ ✿ ✿
CHILDREN: ✿ ✿ ✿ ✿
DIFFICULTY: ✿
SOLITUDE: ✿ ✿
DISTANCE: 5 miles
HIKING TIME: 2–3 hours

GREEN TRAILS MAP: Bonneville Dam 429
OUTSTANDING FEATURES: *Access point to Table Mountain; a good early-season hike close to Portland and Vancouver, and a chance to grab some good grub at one of the many cafés, wineries, and brew pubs that line the streets of Hood River*

otherwise compromised). The hike is accessible for able-bodied children (a one-star rating would denote that only the most gung-ho and physically fit children should go). One star for difficulty indicates it is a very easy hike (five stars would be strenuous). And you can expect to encounter people on the trail (you may well be elbowing your way up the trail on one-star hikes).

Distances given are absolute, but hiking times are estimated using an average hiking speed of 2 to 3 miles per hour, with time built in for pauses at overlooks and brief rests. Overnight hiking times account for the effort of carrying a backpack.

Following this summary information is a brief description of the hike. A more detailed account follows in which trail junctions, stream crossings, and trailside features are noted, along with their distance from the trailhead. Flip through the book, read the brief descriptions, and choose a hike that appeals to you.

Weather

WHEN MOST PEOPLE THINK OF WASHINGTON, the word *rain* usually comes to mind. The truth is, Washington weather is actually quite varied. West of the Cascade Crest, it is mild, with average temperatures ranging from the mid-70s in the summer to the mid-40s in the winter. The official rainy season begins in November and lasts through

April. Weather east of the crest has a much warmer summer, with average temperatures in the 90s. In the winter, snow levels drop to around 1,500 feet and temperatures dip into the low 20s. Occasionally, the difference in these two climates is dramatic, with bluebird skies in the east and a thick, dark wall of clouds hovering directly on the crest.

What does all this mean for the mountains in Washington? Lots and lots of snow! Some of the heaviest snowfall in the Lower 48 occurs on the PCT. While snow enthusiasts are ecstatic about this fact, avid hikers scurry from trailhead to trailhead to cram as much hiking in as possible before the snowflakes fly. To take full advantage of a hiking season in the Cascade Mountains, consider the pros and cons of where to go and when to head out.

MAY–JUNE: *Lasting Sunsets and Lingering Snow*

As the days get longer and the temperature gets warmer, many hikers itch with anticipation to hit the trails. While hiking in June is not uncommon, be prepared for an adventure because lingering snowfields, downed trees, washed-out bridges, and high-river crossings are just a few of the challenges you may encounter. Before heading out, research trail conditions. If you find the high country still snowbound, consider exploring the southern trails of the PCT that lie at a lower elevation or ones that run east of the crest, where the weather is a bit warmer and drier.

JULY–AUGUST: *Blooming Flowers and Buzzing Bugs*

These are by far the most popular months to hike. The weather is warm (although I was snowed on three times in August one summer), the meadows show off their vibrant array of wildflowers, and many of the alpine lakes are just getting warm enough to swim in. The only drawbacks are sharing the trails with other Northwest hikers and escaping from the buzzing, biting insects that swarm the hillsides this time of year. Longer loops into alpine country are a great option during these hot summer months.

Fall in the high country is a special time of year. Cold, crisp nights turn entire hillsides into a canvas of warm colors, including the deep, rich reds of the huckleberry bush and the golden yellow of the larch. It is a quiet, peaceful time to be in the mountains but also a time in which you need to be prepared for overnight temperatures below freezing and rapidly changing weather. If you're worried about weather, take advantage of the number of day hikes along the PCT.

Weather in Washington can be finicky, to say the least. Before every backcountry outing, check a detailed mountain weather forecast—and if it says anything other than *sunny*, prepare for it all.

Water

HOW MUCH IS ENOUGH? One simple physiological fact should convince you to err on the side of excess when deciding how much water to pack: A hiker working hard in 90°F heat needs approximately ten quarts of fluid per day. That's 2.5 gallons—12 large water bottles or 16 small ones. Pack along one or two bottles even for short hikes.

Some hikers and backpackers hit the trail prepared to purify water found along the route. This method, while less dangerous than drinking it untreated, comes with risks. Purifiers with ceramic filters are the safest. Many hikers pack along the slightly distasteful tetraglycine-hydroperiodide tablets to clean water (sold under the names Potable Aqua, Coughlan's, etc.).

Probably the most common waterborne "bug" that hikers ingest is *giardia*, which may not affect you until one to four weeks after you drink the tainted water. When it does hit, it will have you living in the bathroom, passing noxious rotten-egg gas, vomiting, and shivering with chills. Other parasites to worry about include *E. coli* and *cryptosporidium*, both of which are harder to kill than *giardia*.

For most people, the pleasures of hiking make carrying water a relatively minor price to pay to remain healthy. If you're tempted to drink "found water," do so only if you understand the risks involved. Better yet, hydrate before your hike, carry (and drink) six ounces of water for every mile you plan to hike, and hydrate after the hike.

Clothing

LET'S FACE IT—the simple days of grabbing a pair of knickers, a button-up shirt, a sturdy pair of boots, and a wool jacket are gone. The outdoor clothing industry has become a hot, trendy market, and attempting to put an outfit together for a day in the backcountry can be downright mind-boggling. Fortunately, there are just a few things to keep in mind when figuring out how to stay warm, dry, and happy in the woods. How you look on the trail is entirely up to you.

There are two basic groups of materials used in today's outdoor clothing: natural fibers and synthetics. Cotton is a natural fiber best left for the car ride home. When wet, cotton can kill by absorbing moisture and robbing the body of heat. Wool, on the other hand, is an amazing natural fiber that insulates when dry, works when wet, and doesn't absorb odor nearly as easily as synthetic materials. If the thought of wool makes you itchy, you haven't tried today's wool products, which are much softer than their predecessors.

The latest and most diverse materials used in today's outdoor clothing, synthetics range from those made of hollow fibers that trap air and heat, to super-tight weaves that allow vapor to pass through but resist water saturation. Gore-Tex, soft shells, and polypropylenes are just a few of the names and words you will hear when talking about synthetic clothing.

Both synthetic and natural fibers work only as well as your ability to manage them, which is why it is extremely important to layer properly. Make sure you have enough cool layers so you don't leave a trail of sweat when climbing to a pass and enough warm layers to enjoy an afternoon sunset from an alpine ridge. Most important, be prepared for the full range of weather. Lightweight, breathable raingear is an essential piece of the layering system when it comes to hiking in the great Northwest. Even if it doesn't rain, a lightweight shell can block chilly wind, trap in heat, and be a lifesaver against a swarm of bloodthirsty mosquitoes.

Equipment

KEEPING UP WITH THE LATEST AND GREATEST ultra-light gizmos and gadgets is not my cup of tea. My husband, on the other hand, can spend hours researching gear before he even sets foot in a store. No matter where you land on the technology spectrum, a few essentials should accompany you on every outdoor adventure.

FOOTWEAR

The most important piece of equipment you will use on the trail is your footwear. A 4-mile day hike can quickly turn into a blister-fillled torture-fest if you don't have the right shoes for the job. Many shoe companies are now making low-top hiking shoes, which are a little stiffer, have beefier tread, and are more water-resistant than a typical running shoe. These shoes work great for long day hikes with a light pack. If you are looking for something with a little more sup-port, try a lightweight hiking boot. These are a good option if you are hiking with a heavy pack, have weak ankles, or are planning to do any off-trail exploring. Regardless of what footwear you choose, make sure you test them out around town or on local trails before you head into the backcountry.

Backpack

If you're in the market for a new backpack, you're in luck. You have probably 100 different styles, colors, and sizes to choose from. Although the task may seem a little overwhelming, the number of options out there allows you to find a pack that meets your specific needs. A pack that fits well won't leave you standing in your living room debating whether or not you should save an ounce by leaving that extra chocolate bar at home. Spend a little more time and money and find a pack that works.

The Ten Essentials

One of the first rules of hiking is to be prepared for anything. The simplest way to be prepared is to carry the ten essentials. In addition to carrying the items listed below, you need to know how to use them, especially the ones involving navigation. Always consider worst-case scenarios like getting lost, hiking back in the dark, suffering broken gear (e.g., a hip strap on your pack breaking or a water filter getting clogged), twisting an ankle, or getting caught in a brutal thunderstorm. The items listed below don't cost a lot, don't take up much room in a pack, and don't weigh much, but they just might save your life.

WATER: Durable bottles and water treatment such as iodine or a filter

MAP: Preferably a topo map and a trail map with a route description

COMPASS: A high-quality compass

FIRST-AID KIT: A good-quality kit that includes instructions

KNIFE: A multi-tool device with pliers is best

LIGHT: A flashlight or headlamp with extra bulbs and batteries

FIRE: Windproof matches or a lighter and fire starter

EXTRA FOOD: You should always have food in your pack when you've finished hiking

EXTRA CLOTHES: Rain protection, warm layers, gloves, and warm hat

SUN PROTECTION: Sunglasses, lip balm, sunblock, and sun hat

SHELTER

For most people, tents are a necessity when it comes to backpacking in the Northwest. Not only do they keep you dry and warm in foul weather, they can also save you from mosquitoes and biting flies. July and August are about the only months in Washington when you can toy with the idea of leaving the tent at home. If you do, bring some type of emergency shelter or bivy sack and a bug net for hanging out and sleeping.

Even if you are just out for the day, bring some type of shelter to keep you out of the elements if something should go wrong. Building a shelter out of bows and limbs may sound romantic, but in an emergency you want something that is going to keep you relatively warm and dry on the shortest notice. Emergency blankets weigh next to nothing and are fairly inexpensive.

A FEW EXTRAS

Here are a few items that might be worth the extra weight.

TREKKING POLES OR A HIKING STICK: A great way to save your knees

REPAIR KIT: Safety pins, duct tape, extra shoelaces, etc.

FLIP-FLOPS OR SANDALS: When hanging out at camp they create less of an impact on fragile vegetation than boots or hiking shoes and nothing feels better than airing out your feet after a long day on the trail.

First-Aid Kit

A TYPICAL FIRST-AID KIT may contain more items than you might think necessary. These are just the basics. Prepackaged kits in waterproof bags (Atwater Carey and Adventure Medical make a variety of kits) are available. Even though there are quite a few items listed here, they pack down into a small space:

Ace bandages or Spenco joint wraps

Antibiotic ointment (*Neosporin or the generic equivalent*)

Ibuprofen or acetaminophen

Band-Aids

Benadryl or the generic equivalent, diphenhydramine (*in case of allergic reactions*)

Blister kit (*like Moleskin or Spenco "Second Skin"*)

Butterfly-closure bandages

Epinephrine in a prefilled syringe (*for people known to have severe allergic reactions to such things as bee stings, usually by prescription only*)

Gauze and compress pads (*one roll and a half dozen 4 x 4 -inch pads*)

Hydrogen peroxide or iodine

Insect repellent

Matches or a pocket lighter

Sunscreen

Whistle (*more effective at signaling rescuers than your voice*)

Hiking with Children

NO ONE IS TOO YOUNG FOR A HIKE. Be mindful, though. Flat, short, and shaded trails are best with an infant. Toddlers who have not quite mastered walking can still tag along, riding on an adult's back in a child carrier. Use common sense to judge a child's capacity to hike a particular trail and always anticipate that the child will tire quickly and need to be carried. A list of hikes suitable for children is provided in Recommended Hikes (see p. xii).

General Safety

TO SOME POTENTIAL MOUNTAIN ENTHUSIASTS, the deep woods seem inordinately dark and perilous. It is the fear of the unknown that causes this anxiety. No doubt, potentially dangerous situations can occur outdoors, but as long as you use sound judgment and prepare yourself before hitting the trail, you'll be much safer in the woods than in most urban areas of the country. It is better to look at a backcountry hike as a fascinating chance to discover the unknown rather than a chance for potential disaster. If you're new to the game, I'd suggest starting out easy and finding a person who knows more to help you out. In addition, here are a few tips to make your trip safer and easier.

- **ALWAYS CARRY FOOD AND WATER,** whether you are planning to go overnight or not. Food will give you energy, help keep you warm, and sustain you in an emergency until help arrives. You never know if there will be a stream nearby when you become thirsty. Bring potable water or treat water before drinking it from a stream. Boil or filter all found water before drinking it.

- **STAY ON DESIGNATED TRAILS.** Most hikers get lost when they leave the path. Even on the most clearly marked trails, there is usually a point where you have to stop and consider what direction to head. If you become disoriented, don't panic. As soon as you think you may be off track, stop, assess your current direction, then retrace your steps to the point where you went astray. Using a map, a compass, and this book, and keeping in mind what you have passed thus far, reorient yourself, and trust your judgment on which way to continue. If you become absolutely unsure of how to continue, return to your vehicle the way you came in. Should you become completely lost and have no idea how to return to the trailhead, remaining in place along the trail and waiting for help is most often the best option for adults and always the best option for children.

- **BE ESPECIALLY CAREFUL WHEN CROSSING STREAMS.** Whether you are fording the stream or crossing on a log, make every step count. If you have any doubt about maintaining your balance on a foot log, ford the stream instead: use a trekking pole or stout stick for balance and face upstream as you cross. If a stream seems too deep to ford, turn back. Whatever is on the other side is not worth risking your life.

- **BE CAREFUL AT OVERLOOKS.** While these areas may provide spectacular views, they are potentially hazardous. Stay back from the edge of outcrops and be absolutely sure of your footing; a misstep can mean a nasty and possibly fatal fall.

- **STANDING DEAD TREES** and storm-damaged living trees pose a real hazard to hikers and tent campers. These trees may have loose or broken limbs that could fall at any time. When choosing a spot to rest or a backcountry campsite, look up.

- **KNOW THE SYMPTOMS OF HYPOTHERMIA.** Shivering and forgetfulness are the two most common indicators of this stealthy killer. Hypothermia can occur at any elevation, even in the summer, especially when the hiker is wearing lightweight cotton clothing. If symptoms arise, get the victim shelter, hot liquids, and dry clothes or a dry sleeping bag.

- **TAKE ALONG YOUR BRAIN.** A cool, calculating mind is the single most important asset on the trail. Think before you act. Watch your step. Plan ahead. Avoiding accidents is the best way to ensure a rewarding and relaxing hike.

- **ASK QUESTIONS.** National and state forest and park employees are there to help. It's a lot easier to ask advice beforehand and it will help you avoid a mishap away from civilization when it's too late to amend an error.

Animal, Plant, and Insect Hazards

THE FOLLOWING LIST IS INTENDED NOT TO SCARE YOU about heading into the mountains, but rather to inform you of potential hazards and advise you on ways to mitigate them. In all likelihood, the only bear or cougar you will encounter is the one pictured on the information board, ticks will choose to cling to plants, and beautiful sunsets will replace memories of biting mosquitoes.

MOSQUITOES AND BITING FLIES

The peak of mosquito season in the Cascades is usually around July. As the snow melts, stagnant water and warm temperatures combine to create the perfect mosquito habitat. The best way to handle these pesky insects is to wear long sleeves, bring a tent with good ventilation, and, as a last resort, use some type of insect repellent.

Mosquitoes are capable of transmitting the West Nile virus, which is most commonly spread from mosquitoes that have fed on an infected bird. The first case of the virus in the United States was reported in 1999, and it was not reported in Washington until 2006. Most people who carry the virus do not get sick. A few people report flulike symptoms and even fewer have severe reactions. If you are feeling ill after being exposed to mosquitoes, see a doctor immediately.

Biting flies are another one of nature's nuisances. Horse and deer flies are large, and their bite delivers a mighty punch that can itch for days. Midges, more commonly referred to as no-see-ums, are tiny and have a vicious, itchy bite. Follow the same precautions as for mosquitoes.

TICKS

Ticks are a nasty little creation found statewide. Blood-feeding parasites, they can transmit diseases. Cases of tick-related illness are few in Washington, but it is more than worthwhile to take the necessary precautions because extracting them from your skin is anything but fun.

The easiest way to avoid a tick bite is to wear tightly woven long-sleeve shirts and light-colored pants so you can easily spot their dark body on your clothing. Also, tuck your shirt into your pants and your pant legs inside your socks or boots. If you are traveling in a tick-heavy area, consider using a tick repellent. Lastly, make sure you do a thorough body check after hiking. When empty of blood, they are extremely hard to spot. Check carefully, especially in warm, dark areas, such as your armpits, groin, head, neck, and ears. Symptoms of tick-related illnesses resemble the flu, so use caution and see a doctor if you feel sick after hiking in tick country.

BEARS

There are two types of bears in Washington, the grizzly and the black. Black bears are the most common of the two and roam throughout the Cascade Mountains. Grizzlies, on the other hand, are rare, and sightings of them are even rarer. They are on Washington's endangered species list, with reports estimating between 10 and 30 grizzly bears living in the northern part of the Cascades.

Most encounters with bears are brief, and you are lucky to catch a glimpse of their rumps waddling away as they run off toward safety. Remember, they are trying to avoid you just as much as you are trying to avoid them. To reduce your chance of an encounter, make plenty of noise when hiking, avoid traveling by yourself, hike with your dog on a leash (dogs may bring out defensive behaviors in bears), cook away from camp, and hang your food at night.

If you do have an encounter with a bear, try your best to remain calm; speak in a calm, firm voice; and slowly walk away. If you are planning to travel in areas frequented by bears, or particularly those areas with grizzlies, you might consider carrying bear spray, which will more than likely remain in its case.

Cougars

If you should ever spot a cougar, feel honored. These timid mammals work hard to remain unseen and sightings are uncommon, especially in the wild. However, people may encounter cougars that have accidentally stumbled into the urban areas that are encroaching on their ever-shrinking habitat.

In the unlikely event you encounter a cougar, remain calm. Speak to the cougar in an assertive voice and try to make yourself look large and intimidating. Do not make any sudden movements and keep your eye on it at all times. If you have children with you, pick them up or move them close to you. If an attack occurs, fight back.

Rattlesnakes

The western rattlesnake prefers a warm, dry climate, such as is found on the eastern slopes of the Cascades. These rattlers hibernate during the winter in large numbers, tucking themselves in rock crevices on south-facing mountainsides. They slowly begin to emerge between

March and May, dispersing to their summer habitats. Like the cougar, these reptiles are shy and prefer to hide from larger animals (including humans) to avoid being preyed on. Bites are extremely rare, and when people are bit, it is usually because they are stupidly trying to cap-

ture the snake. If you hear a rattle, know that the snake is just letting you know you're entering its territory.

POISONOUS EDIBLES

Berries, mushrooms, and other edible plants thrive throughout Washington. These tasty, natural treats are a true delight, but if you have *any* doubt as to whether a plant is safe to eat, stick to your trail mix.

POISON OAK AND IVY

These rash-producing plants are notorious for ruining a fun outing. Fortunately for those interested in exploring the PCT, the plants have a difficult time growing above 4,000 feet. Unfortunately, many of the PCT access trails begin much lower than that. Being aware of these poisonous plants is key to having a safe, rash-free outing.

POISON OAK

Poison oak has three oaklike leaflets, grows as a vine or shrub, and is the most common rash-producing plant in Washington. Poison ivy has three leaflets and can be a climbing or low-lying vine.

POISON IVY

The body's reaction to the plants' oil, called urushiol, results in swelling, redness, blisters,

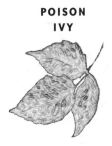

and intense itching. Avoiding contact is the most effective way to avoid a rash. If you have a reaction, don't scratch. Dirty fingernails can cause sores to become infected. Oil-contaminated objects will continue to cause a reaction for at least a year, so thoroughly wash everything that may have the oil on it, including clothing, boots, and pets.

Tips for Enjoying the Pacific Crest Trail in Washington

GIVE YOURSELF PLENTY OF TIME TO ENJOY AN AREA. Washington is a large state, and many of the trailheads along the PCT are in remote areas. The last thing you want to do is spend an entire day in the car only to find that you have to practically run the trail to finish in time. Many of the hikes in a given region in this book leave from the same location or are a short drive from one another. Plan an extended weekend so you can truly enjoy these areas. I found that giving myself enough time allowed me to discover things I would have overlooked, from hidden alpine lakes to isolated backcountry camps. Having a little extra time also lets you check out some of the small mountain towns scattered among the foothills of the PCT.

Ever heard the saying, "Slow and steady gets the turtle to the top?" It's a little mantra I learned from my high school cross-country coach, and it's one I find myself muttering when I have to climb a pass or hike a long distance. The tendency for many of us is to over-exert ourselves by attempting to get a steep hill or series of switchbacks over with as quickly as possible. These sprints will force you to stop every five minutes to catch your breath and will leave you sweat-drenched by the time you reach your destination. To avoid overdoing it, pace yourself and enjoy your surroundings. For long climbs, plan a break every hour or so and hydrate and refuel each time you stop.

When you do finally make it to the top, reward yourself with a "hill pill," such as a chunk of chocolate or a gooey piece of caramel.

As every Pacific Northwesterner knows, it is important to take advantage of good weather in Washington. Most of us, however, do not control our schedules, and it isn't surprising for our days off to coincide with a forecast that calls for "mostly to partly cloudy with a chance of showers." While not ideal, this kind of weather has its perks. The crowds are quieter, the hiking temperature is cooler, and there is nothing more beautiful than watching clouds pour over a jagged ridgeline at sunset. While it's not advisable to go out in a blizzard in June or a severe thunderstorm in July, a little drizzle shouldn't keep you indoors all weekend. Of course, if you do head out in less than ideal weather, plan accordingly by reading a detailed weather forecast and bring all the necessary clothing and equipment to do so safely.

Backcountry Advice

IF THERE IS ONE PIECE OF ADVICE I WOULD GIVE HIKERS, it's plan ahead and prepare. Whether it's the first time you've set foot in a wilderness area or the 500th time, doing a little homework before you hit the trail will ensure you get the most out of your backcountry experience.

- **VERIFY WEATHER CONDITIONS** before you leave home. Access, particularly in Washington, can be a nightmare come spring when the snow begins to melt and the damage of winter is revealed. Throughout winter and spring, avalanches rip from mountainsides, knocking over large, old-growth trees as if they were matchsticks. Heavy spring rains and upper-elevation snowmelt floods rivers and creates landslides, washing out vital sections of trails, roads, and bridges. Local forest and park service ranger stations have a wealth of information on current conditions that will help get you going in the right direction.

- **CAREFULLY REVIEW LAND-ACCESS REGULATIONS.** Once you have determined where you want to go, the next step is figuring out the rules and regulations that apply there. As you will quickly learn, each agency differs in how they manage public lands. For example, you must have a Northwest Forest Pass to park at many forest service trailheads, and Mount Rainier National Park charges an entrance fee, although North Cascades National Park is free.

- **MAKE ARRANGEMENTS IN ADVANCE** for backcountry camping. Backcountry-camping permits and rules also vary among agencies. North Cascades National Park, Mount Rainier National Park, and the Alpine Lakes Wilderness Area require you to register and to camp only at designated campsites. Dogs are not permitted on trails in national parks and in some wilderness areas. As you can see, remembering the rules and regulations can be challenging. To assist you in planning your trip, there is a contact list for each hike in the back of this book.

- **TRAVEL AND CAMP ON DURABLE SURFACES.** To help minimize your impact, camp in designated campsites when they are available. If you are camping in areas without sites, look for places that others have clearly already used and camp on surfaces that are durable, such as grass, rock, dirt, or snow. Avoid camping and hiking in fragile alpine meadows.

- **DISPOSE OF WASTE PROPERLY.** Pack it in; pack it out. Make sure to take all trash, including toilet paper and hygiene products, with you when you go. Human waste should be buried at least 200 feet from water sources, camps, and trails in a cathole six to eight inches deep. Cover your hole with plenty of dirt and disguise it with needles and leaves when you are finished.

- **MINIMIZE CAMPFIRE IMPACTS.** Campfires, particularly in the backcountry, are unnecessary these days, especially with the wide assortment of lightweight stoves available for cooking. If you do decide to build a fire, research restrictions for the area you're visiting. They are often not permitted near lakes, in high-use areas or alpine zones, or when bans are in effect.

Trail Etiquette

WHEN IT COMES TO TRAIL ETIQUETTE, keep in mind that it's the small stuff that counts. While you may not initially see the problem with trampling a lupine or feeding a chipmunk, over time these actions have great effects on the environment. The following tips describe just a few ways you can help ensure that future generations will continue to enjoy the wildness of the wilderness.

- **APPRECIATE WILDLIFE FROM A DISTANCE.** If you are fortunate enough to see wildlife, try to avoid spooking or startling it by quietly observing from a safe distance. Keep your food away from animals by storing it securely and making sure no scraps are left behind. Camp at least 200 feet from water sources so that wildlife have constant access to drinking water.

- **BE AWARE OF THOSE AROUND YOU.** Most hikers are looking to get away from the hustle and bustle of everyday life—respect their wishes by giving them plenty of space and keeping loud noises to a minimum. Also, try to leave an area in its natural state so that others may enjoy it.

- **TREAD LIGHTLY.** Keep to existing trails whenever possible, especially near lakes or campsites. Avoid blazing new paths, further contributing to the maze of social trails (undesignated trails people create over time to access water, check out a viewpoint, get to a campsite, and so on) in these areas. A lot of hard work and money went into creating these amazing trails, so do your part by respecting closures or areas that are being restored.

- **DON'T PICK THE FLOWERS.** Wildflowers, particularly those in alpine environments, have a very short growing season and are, therefore, easily destroyed. *Please* avoid walking, camping, resting, eating, kneeling, or napping on these fragile gems.

Relaxing along the shores of Mig Lake (Hike 19)

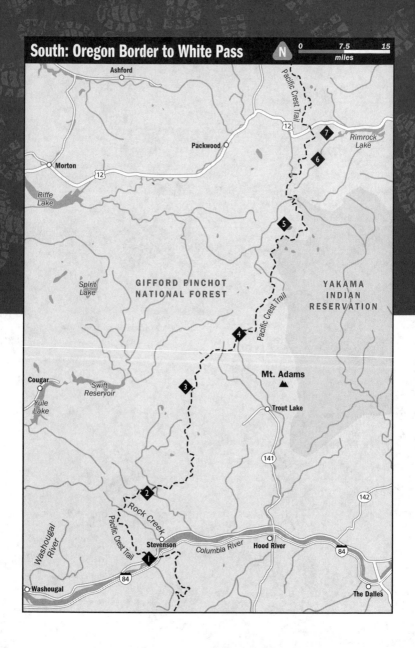

0   7.5   15
miles

Ashford

Pacific Crest Trail

12

7

Rimrock Lake

Packwood

6

Morton

12

Riffe Lake

5

Spirit Lake

GIFFORD PINCHOT NATIONAL FOREST

Pacific Crest Trail

YAKAMA INDIAN RESERVATION

4

3

Mt. Adams

Cougar

Swift Reservoir

Yule Lake

Trout Lake

141

2

142

Rock Creek

Pacific Crest Trail

84

Stevenson

Columbia River

Hood River

84

1

Washougal River

Washougal

The Dalles

1

SOUTH

OREGON BORDER TO
WHITE PASS

1 Gillette Lake *(page 24)*
2 Bunker Hill *(page 29)*
3 Lemei Lake *(page 34)*
4 Horseshoe Meadow *(page 41)*
5 Nannie Ridge *(page 46)*
6 Old Snowy Mountain *(page 51)*
7 Round Mountain *(page 58)*

1 Gillette Lake

SCENERY: ✿ ✿	HIKING TIME: *2–3 hours*
TRAIL CONDITION: ✿ ✿ ✿	GREEN TRAILS MAP: Bonneville Dam 429
CHILDREN: ✿ ✿ ✿ ✿	OUTSTANDING FEATURES: *Access point to*
DIFFICULTY: ✿	*Table Mountain, a good early-season hike close to*
SOLITUDE: ✿ ✿	*Portland and Vancouver, and a chance to grab some*
DISTANCE: *5 miles*	*good grub at one of the many cafés, wineries, and brew*
	pubs that line the streets of Hood River

Although not the most aesthetic hike that runs along the Pacific Crest Trail (PCT) in Washington, it is one of the first to melt out in the spring and its proximity to Portland and Vancouver makes it an easy half-day getaway. This trail is also the access point for Table Mountain, one of the more prominent features on the Washington side of the Columbia River Gorge.

🚶🚶 This hike can begin a couple of ways. Those interested in hiking on the PCT the entire time can begin from a small parking pulloff just south of the Bridge of the Gods on Highway 14 (look for the large Pacific Crest Trail sign). This option adds 1.4 miles to the overall hike and begins on an old, somewhat overgrown power line road that parallels the highway. In a little less than a mile, the trail works its way up a couple of switchbacks before joining Tamanous Trail, your second option for beginning this hike.

Tamanous Trail is the standard approach for Gillette Lake and begins from the well-established Bonneville Trailhead, as shown on the map on page 25. The hike leaves from the far end of the lot, making a leisurely ascent on a well-trodden trail. In less than 0.25 miles, there is a nice view of the Columbia River. A short distance on, the trail turns north and gains a small ridge, where an abandoned clear-cut offers open views to the northwest.

A half mile from the trailhead, the path intersects the PCT. From this junction, head north. Approximately 0.1 mile on, you should see a small pond tucked in a stand of trees when you look

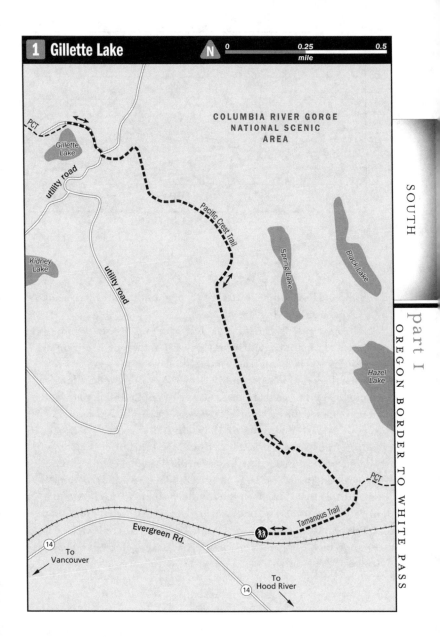

N

0   0.25   0.5
        mile

COLUMBIA RIVER GORGE
NATIONAL SCENIC
AREA

PCT

Gillette
Lake

utility road

Pacific Crest Trail

Kidney
Lake

utility road

Spring Lake

Black Lake

SOUTH

Hazel
Lake

part I
OREGON BORDER TO WHITE PASS

PCT

Tamanous Trail

Evergreen Rd.

(14)
To
Vancouver

To
Hood River
(14)

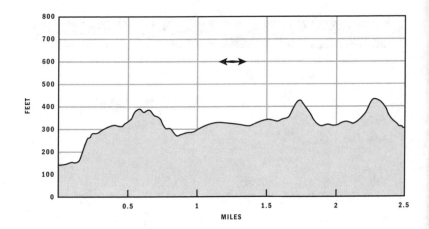

downslope. These ponds, scattered throughout the area, are easy to miss if you aren't paying attention.

The next mile is a mixture of clear-cuts and forests—a good reminder of what the majority of this area would look like if numerous conservation groups had not worked hard to preserve much of the land around the Columbia Gorge. As you meander along, you might also notice that there is a mix of public and private land through this section. The property owners have allowed access, so please be respectful and stay on the main trail.

In 1.3 miles the trail enters a thick forest that offers welcome shade on a hot summer day. As you stroll along, take note of the fern-covered knolls and large mossy boulders, remnants of a massive landslide that tore down the southern slopes of Table Mountain between 250 and 900 years ago. The slide traveled more than 5.5 miles on its journey to the Columbia River, where it created a 200-foot-high earthen dam. Native Americans referred to the site as "Bridge of the Gods."

Spring flowers line the banks of Gillette Lake.

In less than 1 mile, the trail climbs slightly before popping you out on a utility road that serves three sets of Bonneville Dam power lines. Try to ignore the loud buzzing noise because the view from here isn't too shabby. Table Mountain's scarred south face looms in the distance, helping you appreciate how big the Bonneville Land- slide actually was.

Pick up the trail to Gillette Lake on the far side of the service road, where you can glimpse the lake's blue-green waters. Continue downhill; just before you reach the lake's seasonal inlet, a spur trail branches off to the left, to a nice shoreline lunch spot. If the lake is busy, there are a couple other good break spots as you head upstream along the inlet.

Although the lake is modest in size, it's a tranquil place to spend an afternoon fishing (the lake is stocked with golden trout), swimming, reading, or just relaxing. Once you're rejuvenated, simply retrace your steps to the trailhead.

For those of you looking for something slightly more ambitious, you can continue up the PCT to West Table Mountain Trail. Be prepared for a long, strenuous day. Table Mountain Trail is 15.8 miles round-trip and gains 3,350 feet, mostly in the last few miles.

If you find yourself with a couple hours to kill but don't quite have the energy to climb Table Mountain, consider taking a self-guided or ranger-led tour of the Bonneville Dam, built in 1938 by the U.S. Army Corps of Engineers and still managed by them. There are visitor centers on the Washington and Oregon sides of the dam. For more information, call (541) 374-8820.

DIRECTIONS FROM PORTLAND: Take I-84 east 40 miles and exit at Cascade Locks (Exit 40). Pay the toll and cross the Columbia River over the Bridge of the Gods to the Washington side. Turn left onto WA 14 and drive 1.5 miles to the well-developed Bonneville Trailhead parking lot, on the right side of the road. (Note: You will pass the PCT trailhead pulloff just after you cross the Bridge of the Gods.)

FROM VANCOUVER: Head east 35 miles on WA 14. After you go through the town of North Bonneville, keep an eye out for the Bonneville Dam, on your right. Just past the dam is the Bonneville Trailhead parking lot, on the left side of the road.

PERMIT Northwest Forest Pass required.

GPS Trailhead Coordinates	1 Gillette Lake
UTM Zone (WGS 84)	10T
Easting	0583256
Northing	5055921
Latitude	N45.651837°
Longitude	W121.931473°

2 Bunker Hill

SCENERY: 🥾	DISTANCE: *3.6 miles*
TRAIL CONDITION: 🥾 🥾 🥾 🥾	HIKING TIME: *2–3 hours*
CHILDREN: 🥾 🥾	GREEN TRAILS MAP: Wind River 397
DIFFICULTY: 🥾 🥾 🥾	OUTSTANDING FEATURES: *Old-growth*
SOLITUDE: 🥾 🥾 🥾 🥾	*Douglas fir trees, a historical interpretive trail, and*
	a chance to stand atop an old volcanic plug

If you're like me, spring in the Pacific Northwest can be an antsy time of year. While you patiently wait for the upper-elevation hikes to melt out, consider burning some energy with an early-season leg burner to the top of Bunker Hill. This steady climb gains 1,200 feet in less than 1.5 miles along a series of switchbacks that zigzag their way up the hillside. Views from the top are limited, but the feeling of accomplishment makes it worth the effort.

🚶🚶 To begin this hike, head north on the PCT through a large meadow bursting with daffodils and dandelions in late spring. As you traverse the meadow, note the large, forested mound ahead. This is Bunker Hill, an igneous volcanic plug that was pushed up through layers of lava flows and volcanic debris 20 to 25 million years ago.

Continue through the meadow and, in less than 0.25 miles, the trail enters a stand of deciduous trees, whose leaves rustle even in the lightest of breezes. In another 0.25 miles the trail reaches the signed turnoff for Bunker Hill. From this point on you will remain in the forest.

Older guidebooks talk of sweeping views from the top of Bunker Hill, probably from when it was still used as a fire lookout, but I ate lunch on the top in a thick stand of second-growth trees with little to no view. As you hike up the hillside, you occasionally catch glimpses of the surrounding ridgelines, but the views are limited.

As you begin your climb up Bunker Hill you will soon see large, old-growth Douglas fir and hemlock trees scattered throughout

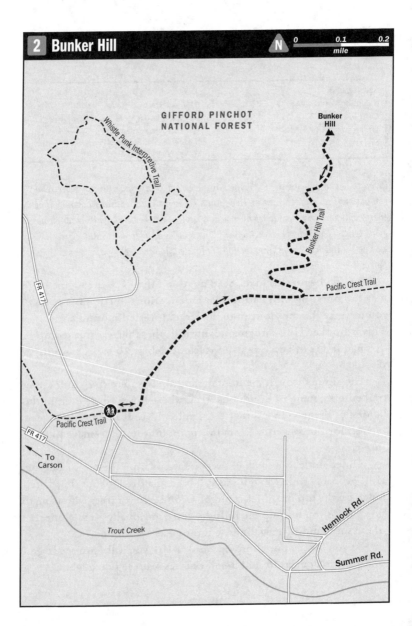

N

0   0.1   0.2
mile

GIFFORD PINCHOT
NATIONAL FOREST

Bunker
Hill

Whistle Punk Interpretive Trail

Bunker Hill Trail

Pacific Crest Trail

FR 417

Pacific Crest Trail

FR 417

To
Carson

Trout Creek

Hemlock Rd.

Summer Rd.

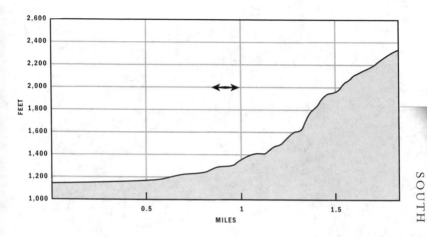

this second-growth forest. The Douglas fir, in particular, played an important role in the history of this area and the way in which the U.S. manages forests today. The Wind River area is just one of 77 experimental forests in the U.S. The Wind River branch was established in 1932; however, Thornton T. Munger, who later became the first director of the Pacific Northwest Research Station, began to conduct the relevant research for the Forest Service back in 1909.

This forest was originally used to study the great Douglas fir forests of the Pacific Northwest, and many of the practices for studying, cultivating, and managing forests were developed during this period. Today the research facility is used primarily to study the ecosystem of Douglas fir forests and research old-growth tree and wildlife habitats.

Continuing your climb, you will notice that the first few switchbacks are relatively long and gradual. In less than 1 mile, the switchbacks tighten up and become a bit steeper as you inch closer to the summit. When you reach the last switchback, at 1.7 miles, you will notice a path that branches off to the right, your only chance to see

A flowering meadow at the base of Bunker Hill

open views of the Wind River valley. Be careful: Getting to this view-point is tricky, and a slip could be fatal. The Forest Service strongly encourages folks to stay on the main trail.

As you hike beyond the viewpoint, the trail makes one last, steep push to the top before reaching the summit of Bunker Hill, elevation 2,383 feet. The big clue that you have reached your final destination is the remnants of an abandoned Forest Service fire lookout. A few foundation blocks are all that remain; they make for a nice place to sit and have lunch. Once you have recovered from your ascent, simply retrace your footsteps the 1.8 miles to the start of the hike.

If you find yourself with a little extra time when you arrive back at the trailhead, check out Whistle Punk Interpretive Trail. To get there, walk 0.25 miles up FR 417 to the trailhead parking area, on the right side of the road. The trail itself travels along a railroad grade that dates to 1913. Informative signs and a brochure tell the story of the Wind River Logging Company and the forest-management practices associated with railroad logging. The trail also wanders through an old-growth forest, an old Wind River Nursery field, and past a wetland area. Choose between the 0.75- or the 1.5-mile loop.

DIRECTIONS   FROM PORTLAND: Drive east 40 miles on I-84 and exit at Cascade Locks. Pay the toll and cross the Columbia River to Washington State over the Bridge of the Gods. Turn right (east) onto WA 14 and follow it to the Carson exit.

FROM VANCOUVER: Drive east 55 miles on WA 14 to the Carson exit.

FROM WA 14: Turn off WA 14 and continue 8.5 miles on Wind River Road to Hemlock Road (you will see a sign for the Wind River Work Center). Turn left on Hemlock and continue 1.5 miles to FR 43. This road is just to the right of the Wind River Work Center and is easy to miss if you are not paying attention. Turn right onto FR 43 and drive 0.5 miles to FR 417. Turn right onto FR 417 and, just as you crest the hill, keep an eye out for the southbound PCT, on the left side of the road (about 100 yards from the turnoff). Continue driving; when the road makes a somewhat sharp turn to the left, you will see the trailhead for the northbound PCT on the right side of the road.

PERMITS   Northwest Forest Pass required.

GPS Trailhead Coordinates	2 Bunker Hill
UTM Zone (WGS 84)	10T
Easting	0582340
Northing	5073215
Latitude	N45.807581°
Longitude	W121.940279°

3 Lemei Lake

SCENERY: ☆ ☆ ☆ ☆
TRAIL CONDITION: ☆ ☆ ☆ ☆
CHILDREN: ☆ ☆ ☆ ☆
DIFFICULTY: ☆ ☆ ☆
SOLITUDE: ☆ ☆ ☆
DISTANCE: *12.5 miles*

HIKING TIME: *6–7 hours or overnight*
GREEN TRAILS MAP: Indian Heaven 365S
OUTSTANDING FEATURES: *Grassy meadows to lounge around in, endless fields of huckleberries, multiple lakes to laze away the afternoon, and a variety of hiking options*

Panoramic views, wide-open fields, and a chance to stand on top of something are usually among my requirements for a good hike. So, when I stumbled across the Indian Heaven Wilderness, I have to admit I was skeptical; how interesting could a series of lakes through the woods really be? But this impressive scenery will keep the most extreme of alpine enthusiasts mesmerized. This hike is best done late summer or early fall, when the berries are ripe, the fields are bursting with color, and the mosquitoes are minimal.

🚶🚶 From the pullout, head south (across the road) to the trailhead, which is well established and easy to find. The trail is flat at the start and almost immediately enters the Indian Heaven Wilderness, an area rich in natural resources. Abundant berries, wild game, and fish have brought a number of Native American tribes to this area for nearly 10,000 years. Many Native Americans continue to uphold their traditions in the Sawtooth Huckleberry Fields, which are some of the most productive huckleberry fields in the Northwest. Situated just east of FR 24, parts of the fields are designated for exclusive use by the Yakama Nation through a handshake agreement with the Forest Service in 1932. As you will probably notice on the hike to Placid Lake, many of the berries here are harvested as well. Not to worry, the entire hike is laden with a variety of huckleberry bushes, providing ample opportunities to sample one of nature's greatest treats.

After a pleasant 0.5-mile stroll through a large stand of timber, you reach the shallow waters of Placid Lake. The gentle descent is a good warm-up for the 1,000-foot climb from the lake up to the

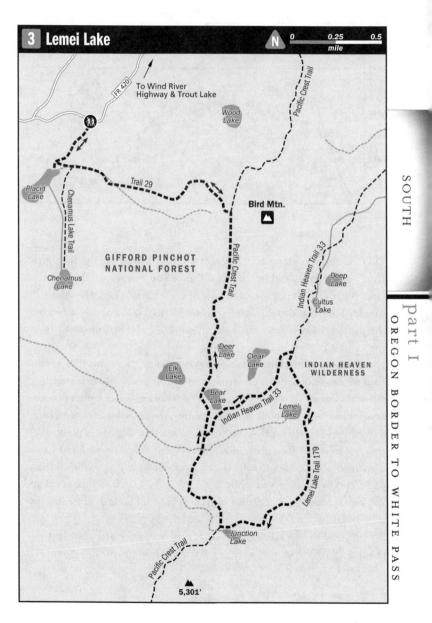

N

0   0.25   0.5
mile

To Wind River
Highway & Trout Lake

FR 420

Wood
Lake

Pacific Crest Trail

Trail 29

Placid
Lake

Chenamus Lake Trail

Bird Mtn.

GIFFORD PINCHOT
NATIONAL FOREST

Pacific Crest Trail

Chenamus
Lake

Indian Heaven Trail 33

Deep
Lake

Cultus
Lake

Deer
Lake

Clear
Lake

INDIAN HEAVEN
WILDERNESS

Elk
Lake

Bear
Lake

Indian Heaven Trail 33

Lemei
Lake

Lemei Lake Trail 179

Pacific Crest Trail

Junction
Lake

▲
5,301'

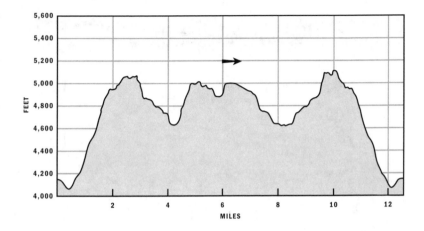

PCT. Continue along the trail as it skirts just up from the southern shore of the lake, and in a short distance you reach a marked junction. Veer left, as the marker indicates, along Trail 29. The path quickly climbs above the lake, and in less than 0.5 miles you reach the junction for Chenamus Lake (Trail 29A). Continue heading east on Trail 29.

From the junction, the trail makes a steady climb through a beautiful forest, alive with an assortment of mushrooms, moss-covered trees, and small flowers. At 1.5 miles the trail reaches a bench that rises above Placid Lake's inlet. By midsummer, the inlet looks more like a small meadow than a flowing creek. In another 0.3 miles the trail passes a group of moss-covered boulders that mark the outlet of a tiny, unnamed pond, one of many in this area. Then it wraps around the pond and drops into a shrubby meadow. A few hundred more feet and you reach a lush grass meadow, a great spot to take a break late in summer or fall, when the ground is dry and the bugs are gone.

Beyond the meadow, the trail continues east-northeast. Just as the thought "Are we there yet?" begins to cross your mind, the trail

Tranquil waters flow out of Lemei Lake in the Indian Heaven Wilderness.

crosses the top of a boulder field, where you are rewarded with a stunning view of the ashy flanks of Mount St. Helens. Take a moment to enjoy the image, as it is the only time you'll see the mystical volcano from the trail. From here it is only a short distance before the trail tops out on a ridge, crossing an open meadow that offers views of Bird Mountain's forested slopes.

From the meadow, the trail reenters the woods and heads southeastward before reaching the PCT at 2.5 miles. Head south and soon reach a small boulder field with a series of murky ponds tucked among tall, green grass to the west of the trail. The trail is somewhat humdrum for the next mile or so. A sign marking the distance to Blue Lake, a popular destination for day and overnight hikers, is about the only significant landmark until you reach the junction for Clear Lake, where you head east, up Indian Heaven Trail 33.

A striking view of Mt. St. Helens

The trail ascends steeply; however, the lake is not far and the path quickly levels out. At first glance, Clear Lake seems like a clear version of a small pond, but as the trail works its way toward the northern shoreline, the lake's long southern shores are slowly revealed. Continuing on, the trail reaches a junction at 4.1 miles. Head south on Lemei Lake Trail 179. Trail 33 goes north to Cultus Lake and on to Cultus Creek Campground, a popular access point for this area.

I have to admit that this is my favorite part of the hike. While the PCT ambles through the forest, Lemei Lake Trail travels through vast open meadows full of low-lying huckleberry bushes.

The chocolate-colored outlet of Lemei Lake is 1.5 miles from the junction with Clear Lake. From this point you can enjoy views of Lemei Peak. As you approach the lake, you will notice that the open terrain, abundant berries, and lack of people combine to create the perfect opportunity to see wildlife, which also makes it a great destination for an overnight. A small knoll above the lake, with plenty of tall trees for hanging food far from greedy paws, makes for a good spot to pitch a tent.

For those continuing on, follow the trail as it makes three steep switchbacks up and out of the Lemei Lake basin. The trail plateaus for a mile and wanders through more spectacular terrain. At 6.3 miles the trail reenters the forest and makes a steep, somewhat rugged descent down to the pleasant waters of Junction Lake. You'll find a good campsite on the southwest shore and a decent one along the northwest shore.

Junction Lake is a fitting name—the junction with the PCT is on the eastern shoreline. Continue north on the PCT, and in 0.5 miles you cross the dry bed of Lemei Creek. Notice the colorful pumice rocks in the streambed, a sign of the area's previous volcanic activity. As you amble through the woods, keep an eye out to the west for the muddy waters of Acker Lake, which is 1 mile or so from the junction. The trail crosses a couple of smaller, dried-up creeks and makes a gradual ascent as it approaches the bluish-green waters of Bear Lake, a popular destination for swimmers, loungers, day hikers, and backpackers. A junction with Elk Lake Trail 176 above the southeast corner of Bear Lake is a good place to access a couple of campsites on the lake's southwest shore.

Take a break at the lake, then continue north on the PCT. In 0.5 miles the trail rounds the east side of Deer Lake, a smaller lake with less-ideal camping than that at Bear. Just past the shoreline, you will rejoin Indian Heaven Trail 33. From here it is 3.5 miles back to the trailhead.

DIRECTIONS   To navigate this confusing area, stop by the Mount Adams Ranger Station (in Trout Lake) or Jack's Restaurant (just outside of Cougar) to get a Mount St. Helens vicinity map. These maps do not show the many Forest Service roads, but they will give you an overall view of the area.

FROM PORTLAND: Head east 40 miles on I-84 to Hood River. Cross the Bridge of the Gods to reach WA 14. Turn west and go 1.5 miles to WA 141, then continue north to Trout Lake. Once there, follow the signs to the Mount Adams Ranger Station. Continue past the ranger station just more than 1 mile and turn right onto FR 88 (from here it is easiest to follow the signs for Mount St. Helens). Drive 13 miles until you reach the Big Tire Junction (you will know when you're there). Veer left onto FR 8851, which becomes FR 24 in 2.5 miles. In another 3.5 miles turn right onto FR 30, which is paved for the first 2.5 miles and then becomes gravel. Continue another 2.7 miles and turn left onto FR 420, which was unmarked at the time of this hike.

FROM SEATTLE: Take I-5 south 153 miles to WA 503. Continue east through the town of Cougar to reach FR 90; turn right (from here it is easiest to follow the signs for Trout Lake). Continue to the turnoff for Curly Creek and turn right again. When you reach a T-intersection, turn left onto the Wind River Highway and continue approximately 3 miles. Veer right onto FR 30, which is gravel. Continue approximately 2 miles and turn right onto FR 420, which was unmarked at the time of this hike. If you reach milepost 38, you have gone too far.

ONCE ON FR 420: Continue 1 mile along FR 420. At the time of this hike, the road was washed out 0.25 miles from the trailhead. While some braves souls may venture on in four-wheel-drive vehicles, it is just as easy to park the car on the shoulder and walk the short distance up the road to the trailhead.

PERMIT   Northwest Forest Pass required. Self-issued permits available at trailhead.

GPS Trailhead Coordinates	3 Lemei Lake
UTM Zone (WGS 84)	10T
Easting	0592128
Northing	5100135
Latitude	N46.048583°
Longitude	W121.809169°

4 Horseshoe Meadow

SCENERY: ✿ ✿ ✿
TRAIL CONDITION: ✿ ✿ ✿ ✿ ✿
CHILDREN: ✿ ✿
DIFFICULTY: ✿ ✿ ✿
SOLITUDE: ✿ ✿ ✿

DISTANCE: *10 miles*
HIKING TIME: *5 hours or overnight*
GREEN TRAILS MAP: Mount Adams 367S
OUTSTANDING FEATURES: *Up-close views of Mount Adams, large grassy meadows to lounge around in and good huckleberry picking in August*

At 12,276 feet, Mount Adams is the second-highest mountain in Washington and the third-highest in the Cascade Range. Yet most Northwesterners have never even been to this amazing wilderness area. Mount Adams is easily overshadowed by its popular neighbors, Mount Rainier National Park and Mount St. Helens National Volcanic Monument. If you want to escape the crowds on a long weekend, check out this often-overlooked Washington gem.

🚶🚶 I am a huge fan of small mountain communities in recreational meccas. So, really, cute, outdoorsy Trout Lake near this hike's trailhead shouldn't have surprised me. Surrounded by miles upon miles of trails and tucked beneath the graceful silhouette of Mount Adams, this small mountain town should be on your list of cool places to visit. Oh yeah, there's lots of great hiking, too.

Once you make it to the trailhead, go north along the PCT and in 0.25 miles you reach a good campsite near a permanent creek. Because there is no water late in the summer elsewhere in this area, you may see PCT thru-hikers and backpackers camped out at this spot. Continue across the bridge, and in another 0.25 miles you reach the Mount Adams Wilderness boundary. The next mile or so is pleasant as the trail winds through the forest, crossing a couple of creeks that can be dry by late summer.

At 1.7 miles, the trail makes a short, steep ascent that will make you appreciate the warm-up you've been enjoying up to this point. After a few hundred feet, the trail levels off and heads eastward

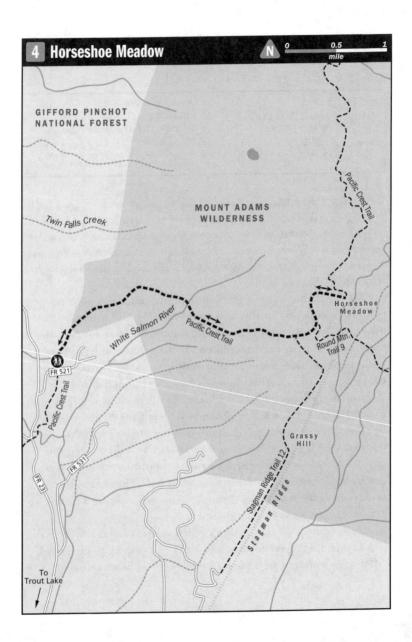

N

0   0.5   1
mile

GIFFORD PINCHOT
NATIONAL FOREST

Twin Falls Creek

MOUNT ADAMS
WILDERNESS

Pacific Crest Trail

White Salmon River

Pacific Crest Trail

Horseshoe
Meadow

FR 521

Round Mtn.
Trail 9

Pacific Crest Trail

FR 531

FR 23

Grassy
Hill

Stagman Ridge Trail 12

Stagman Ridge

To
Trout Lake

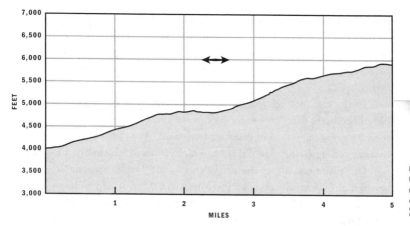

through an open stand where waist-high huckleberry bushes cover the forest floor. At approximately 2.5 miles the trail descends slightly as it crosses the usually dry White Salmon River, more of a small stream. Just before the trail switchbacks (approximately 100 yards from the crossing) a spring 50 yards below the trail is a good source for water.

Once you round the switchback, the trail turns north and the forest becomes thick as you cross the indiscernible river again. At 3.2 miles the trail makes another turn to the east, and in 0.3 miles it passes an overhanging boulder that would barely shelter one small person. This boulder also marks the entry into the subalpine, where low-lying huckleberry bushes interlaced with bunches of lupine cover the ground.

The trail descends gradually as it snakes through small meadows and stands of Douglas fir and mountain hemlock. At 4.2 miles you cross a small boulder with a flat top, a great spot for a break to appreciate your first good view of Mount Adams, perfectly framed. You can't help but wonder if the boulder was intentionally placed.

Just past this spot is an eye-catching meadow with a large rock outcropping that looks as if one side of it was hit with a gigantic hammer and broken into hundreds of pieces. Logs have been placed in the trail that leads into the meadow to keep people from trampling this fragile area. Not to worry—there are plenty of other good places, with heartier vegetation and more spectacular scenery, to take a break.

As the trail rounds the meadow it eventually passes another jumble of boulders that has been overrun with huckleberry bushes, which seem to grow out of every crack and crevasse. At 4.7 miles the trail intersects Stagman Ridge Trail 12, which heads south toward FR 120.

Continue east along the PCT, and in 0.25 miles you reach another junction with Round the Mountain Trail 9. If you head southeast along this trail, past the unmarked wooden post with the carved tip, you will soon arrive at Dry Lake Camp. (Take note of the name and pack in water if you are interested in camping at the meadow.) Views of both the mountain and Horseshoe Meadow are excellent from this location.

If you have energy to burn, add a nice 4.3-mile loop to your hike by following Trail 9 east to where it joins Trail 9A. Follow it downhill to Looking Glass Lake, a quaint lake nestled in the trees with a view of Mount Adams from the southwest shore. Finish the loop by continuing northwest to the junction with the PCT.

For those interested in exploring the PCT from the junction, the trail makes a sharp bend as it skirts the meadow where Mount Adams White Salmon Glacier can be seen clinging to the crumbly, pumice slopes that seem to be holding the mountain together. The view disappears as the trail begins a short climb to the northwest. As the trail follows the west side of the ridge, you can see Mount Rainier to the northwest, which makes the extra elevation gain worth the effort. A series of large flat boulders, 0.7 miles from the junction, mark a nice alpine setting to have lunch and call it a day. If you feel overly motivated or want to do an out-and-back overnight trip, continue another 3 miles to reach the shallow, murky waters of Sheep Lake.

Mt. Adams's White Salmon Glacier as seen from Horseshoe Meadow

DIRECTIONS   Head east from Portland 40 miles on I-84 to Hood River. Cross the Bridge of the Gods to WA 14. Turn west and drive 1.5 miles to WA 141, then continue north to Trout Lake. Once there, continue to follow WA 141. In a few miles the road splits; take the left branch onto FR 23 and follow it 14 miles until you see a sign for the PCT on the left side of the road. Turn right onto FR 521. Follow the road approximately 0.5 miles and park in the pullout on the left side of the road.

PERMIT   Northwest Forest Pass required. Self-issued permits available at trailhead.

GPS Trailhead Coordinates	4 Horseshoe Meadow
UTM Zone (WGS 84)	10T
Easting	0606026
Northing	5113929
Latitude	N46.170686°
Longitude	W121.626494°

5 Nannie Ridge

SCENERY: ☆ ☆ ☆ ☆	HIKING TIME: *1–2 days*
TRAIL CONDITION: ☆ ☆ ☆ ☆	GREEN TRAILS map: *Walupt Lake 335*
CHILDREN: ☆ ☆	OUTSTANDING FEATURES: *A small alpine lake*
DIFFICULTY: ☆ ☆ ☆	*surrounded by fields of wildflowers, with fabulous*
SOLITUDE: ☆ ☆ ☆	*views of the Goat Rocks and Mount Adams; a loop*
DISTANCE: *14.5 miles*	*hike through scenic high country; and lots of great*
	swimming holes to cool off in

If you want to explore the Goat Rocks Wilderness but don't have time to make it all the way into the heart of the mountains, check out the sweeping views from the flowery meadows along Nannie Ridge. Depending on where you live, the drive to Walupt Creek Campground can be long, so make a weekend of it by car camping and completing the loop as a long day hike—or better yet, spend a night in the high country. A word of caution: If you visit this area in the fall, make sure you and your four-legged companion wear bright colors; the area is popular with hunters.

🚶🚶 From the northwest corner of Walupt Lake (elevation 3,930 feet), follow painted horseshoes (a sign of this area's popularity with horsepackers) to the trailhead for Walupt Creek Trail 101. You'll reach Nannie Ridge Trail 98 within the first few hundred feet. Take it and slowly and steadily climb 2,000 feet.

The first 1.5 miles of the hike are fairly mundane. The trail travels through thick, forested slopes with little to no views up a north-trending path. At 1.7 miles, the forest slowly begins to open as you continue your ascent into the high country, and for the first time you can see the stubby profile of Mount St. Helens to the southwest.

After a series of switchbacks, at 2.5 miles the trail tops out on a spur ridge that comes off the south side of Nannie Peak. If you are looking for a short excursion, you'll find great views by hiking 0.5 miles along an abandoned trail to the 6,106-foot summit of Nannie Peak. The trail is obvious and heads north from the ridge.

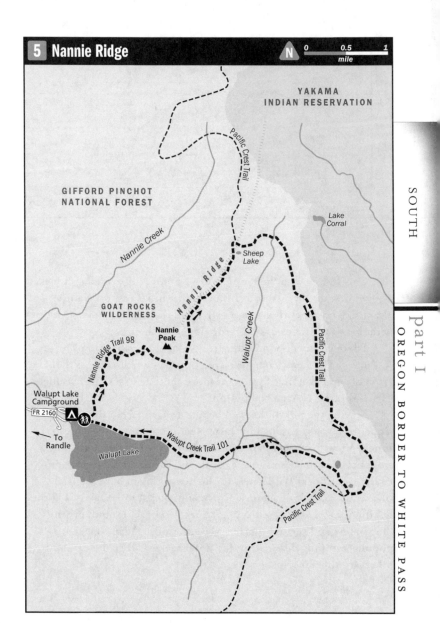

YAKAMA
INDIAN RESERVATION

GIFFORD PINCHOT
NATIONAL FOREST

Lake
Corral

Nannie Creek

Nannie Ridge

Sheep
Lake

GOAT ROCKS
WILDERNESS

Pacific Crest Trail

Nannie Ridge Trail 98

Nannie
Peak

Walupt Creek

Pacific Crest Trail

Walupt Lake
Campground

FR 2160

To
Randle

Walupt Lake

Walupt Creek Trail 101

Pacific Crest Trail

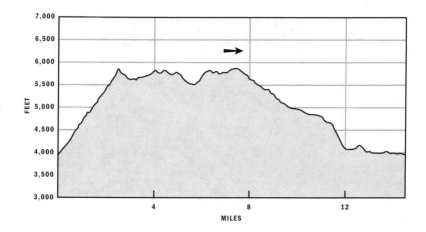

Continuing with the loop, follow Nannie Ridge Trail as it makes a slight descent, bypassing a cliff band that heads east off Nannie Peak. The craggy cliffs are impressive and their color contrasts nicely with that of the fields of blooming flowers at their base.

There is a small pond with a couple of reasonable campsites at 3.3 miles. The views from here are not nearly as stunning as they are from Sheep Lake, but if you want more solitude or a short overnight excursion, this is not a bad option.

Leaving the pond, the trail begins a slight ascent through open slopes to a grassy saddle and the perfect place for an afternoon lunch. Views from here are fantastic, with the glaciated, gleaming slopes of Mount Adams to the south and the dry, arid mountains of the Goat Rocks Wilderness to the north. From here the trail pleasantly rolls along Nannie Ridge and, at 4.5 miles, arrives at the quaint Sheep Lake (elevation 5,710 feet), whose tranquil green-blue waters and picture-perfect view of Mount Adams make it a popular camping destination for horsepackers, thru-hikers, and hikers on shorter trips.

A gorgeous summer day at Sheep Lake

Soon after you leave the lake on the Nannie Ridge Trail, you reach a junction with the PCT. Follow the southbound trail around Sheep Lake toward the head of the Walupt Creek basin, where great views stretch to the south down the Walupt Creek valley.

The trail now descends through a mix of open and semi-forested slopes. Around 8.5 miles you spy the deep-blue water of Walupt Lake to the southwest. The trail continues to drop, and at 10 miles arrives at two small lakes that sit below Lakeview Mountain (elevation 6,660 feet) and the junction with Walupt Creek Trail 101. Head west on the trail as it skirts the small lakes, passing several nice campsites.

After cresting a ridge you begin a steep descent down tight switch-backs along a narrow ridgeline with creeks running on either side. The small amount of water that drains through this area creates a lush environment flourishing with ferns, vanilla leaf, and foamflower.

Two miles or so from the PCT turnoff, the trail crosses Walupt Creek. There are a couple of good campsites near the creek; however, there may not be any water late in the season. Continue on through stands of Douglas fir, and in another mile you reach Walupt Lake's inlet creek. The last stretch follows the northern shoreline of the lake, a great place to stroll with kids if you are staying at the Walupt Lake Campground and looking for a brief outing. In another mile the trail reaches the turnoff for Nannie Ridge and in a few hundred feet arrives back at the trailhead.

DIRECTIONS From Randle, follow US 12 east 13 miles to the turnoff for Johnson Creek on FR 21 (the turnoff is 2.5 miles west of Packwood). Turn right (north) and follow the road 16 miles to the turnoff for FR 2160. Turn left and drive approximately 5 more miles to Walupt Creek Campground and park in the day-use area. Follow painted horseshoes to the trailhead.

PERMIT Northwest Forest Pass required. Self-issued permits available at trailhead.

GPS Trailhead Coordinates	5 Nannie Ridge
UTM Zone (WGS 84)	10T
Easting	0617574
Northing	5142208
Latitude	N46.423210°
Longitude	W121.469873°

6 Old Snowy Mountain

SCENERY: ✿ ✿ ✿ ✿ ✿	DISTANCE: *26 miles*
TRAIL CONDITION: ✿ ✿ ✿	HIKING TIME: *2–3 days*
CHILDREN: ✿	GREEN TRAILS MAP: White Pass 303
DIFFICULTY: ✿ ✿ ✿ ✿	OUTSTANDING FEATURES: *Breathtaking*
SOLITUDE: ✿ ✿ ✿	*views, "airy" sections of trail, alpine meadows, ancient glaciers, and a walk-up summit*

When I chat with Northwest natives about Goat Rocks Wilderness, they often remark: "I've always wanted to go there." Well, go ahead and set foot in this awe-inspiring area, a favorite section for many PCT thru-hikers. The upper slopes of this hike can be snowbound well through July, so an ice axe and crampons may be necessary.

🚶🚶 Prepare for two things on this hike—jaw-dropping beauty and having to work for it. The trail begins at the rippling waters of North Fork Tieton and gains approximately 4,000 feet in 13 miles on its journey to the windswept summit of Old Snowy Mountain. If the distance or elevation seems daunting, there is an alternative approach from the much more popular southern route through Snowgrass Flats (cutting the distance in half). That said, the extra energy it takes to do the hike from this approach dramatically cuts the amount of traffic, and the trail leading to Old Snowy from the north will take your breath away.

The trail begins by immediately crossing North Fork Tieton River, more of a small creek than a raging river by late summer or fall. On the other side of the bridge, you enter Goat Rocks Wilderness, in which you will remain for the duration of the hike. In less than 0.25 miles, you reach a junction. Take the right branch on Trail 1118 toward Tieton Pass. The other trail travels southeast on its long climb to Bear Creek Mountain.

From the junction, the trail gradually ascends, crossing a few small creeks along the way. At 1 mile, you reach a charming stream that

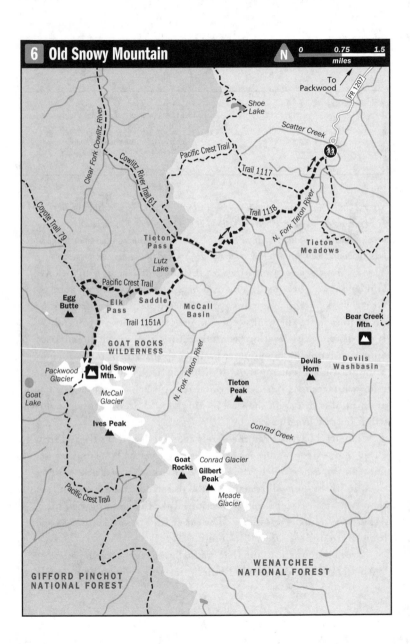

N

0   0.75   1.5
miles

To
Packwood

FR 1207

Shoe
Lake

Scatter Creek

Clear Fork Cowlitz River

Cowlitz River Trail 61

Pacific Crest Trail

Trail 1117

Trail 1118

Coyote Trail 79

N. Fork Tieton River

Tieton
Meadows

Tieton
Pass

Lutz
Lake

Pacific Crest Trail

Egg
Butte

Elk
Pass

Saddle

McCall
Basin

Trail 1151A

Bear Creek
Mtn.

GOAT ROCKS
WILDERNESS

Packwood
Glacier

Old Snowy
Mtn.

Devils
Horn

Devils
Washbasin

Goat
Lake

McCall
Glacier

N. Fork Tieton River

Tieton Peak

Ives Peak

Conrad Creek

Pacific Crest Trail

Goat
Rocks

Conrad Glacier

Gilbert
Peak

Meade
Glacier

WENATCHEE
NATIONAL FOREST

GIFFORD PINCHOT
NATIONAL FOREST

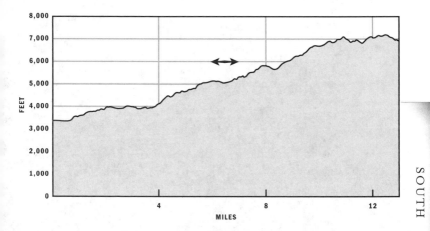

pours down a hanging garden, then crosses the trail into a marshland full of vibrant, green horsetails. Just beyond here, you arrive at Trail 1117, a faint path easily overlooked if it weren't for the sign marking it. This trail takes off to the west and in 2.5 miles reaches the PCT 3 miles south of Tieton Pass. Remain on Trail 1118's more defined path, which gets you into Goat Rocks faster.

The trail continues its climb and is fairly ho-hum as it works its way through the woods before cresting a ridge 2.5 miles from the trailhead, your first real opportunity for open views. Devils Horns, Bear Creek Mountain, and Tieton Peak reveal themselves to the south, and as you drop back into the forest, knowing that the views are only going to improve, you might find a little pep in your step.

Another 1.5 miles brings you to the forested saddle of Tieton Pass, elevation 4,800 feet. The pass sits at a three-way junction, with the PCT running north and south and Cowlitz River Trail branching off to the northwest. Follow the PCT south as the trail meanders up, over, and around ribs, ridges, and small knolls. At 1.5 miles from Tieton Pass, you reach the shallow waters of Lutz

Scoping out the PCT on the way to Old Snowy Mountain

Lake, a good place to camp, especially if you are traveling in a large group. It does make for a fairly long day hike to the summit of Old Snowy, but it also means not having to travel any farther with a heavy pack.

The trail skirts the lake and then begins a mellow climb to the turnoff for the wet meadows of McCall Basin, a popular spot to pitch a tent, especially for hunters who come here in the fall when the high hunt is open. If you are looking to escape some of the crowds (which aren't much of a problem out here) and the weather is decent, continue another mile or 2, to sites above tree line.

From the junction, the trail ascends a couple switchbacks then travels up a drainage with excellent views down into McCall Basin and southeast toward Tieton Peak. Just a couple more switchbacks and you're close to a saddle with a campsite tucked in a small stand of trees. The site provides a fairly nice shelter and could work in a pinch, but there is no water and there are better sites farther up the trail. Just beyond the saddle, the trail crests the ridge and offers up views to the northwest, where you can catch a glimpse of Mount Rainier. The vista quickly disappears as the trail crosses back over to the south side of the ridge, working its way slightly below the summit of an unnamed knoll.

As the trail approaches a broad saddle, it is hard not to be moved by the beauty of this place, where hanging glaciers, cascading creeks, fields of wildflowers, and ancient peaks dominate the landscape. The trail descends from the saddle through a stand of alpine fir and hemlock, into a large basin. Just before the trail begins a steep climb, keep an eye out for a spur trail that takes off toward the creek, with a couple good campsites in a stand of trees near the water. This area is fragile, so please use existing sites, and established trails to access them.

Continuing from the basin, the trail zigzags up a narrow rib and tops out at 6,000 feet on an expansive plateau. The path from here can be somewhat hard to follow because you have to cross creeks and snow patches along the way. A number of painted cairns every few hundred feet help ensure you are going the right way. There are tent sites (the last until the west flank of Old Snowy) scattered across the plateau; however, if the weather is poor, these sites will provide only minimal protection against the elements.

Moving along, the trail skirts a pyramid-shaped peak, where water has carved deep channels through the reddish-brown rock. To the west lies the Elk Pass snowfield, where you can sometimes see the boot tracks of hikers who glissaded through the snow. From here the main trail takes you across glacially striated bedrock before it ascends to a saddle just below Peak 6768.

The trail traverses below the peak's rugged ridgeline, crossing the exposed north face, where snow can linger well into summer. The scene from here is spectacular, with the Clear Fork of the Cowlitz River canyon to the north and the gleaming slopes of Mount Rainier in the distance. The trail continues to wrap around to the southwest and soon enters a stand of weather-beaten white bark pines. As you exit the stand of trees you arrive at Elk Pass (elevation 6,700 feet) and enter the heart of Goat Rocks Wilderness.

From the pass, Coyote Trail 79 branches off toward Upper Lake Creek canyon, which funnels water from all of the steep creeks and long, narrow waterfalls that pour from the snowfields above. Continue south on the PCT along an exciting section of trail constructed in 1953 and 1954. As you resume your hike from the pass, the trail works its way up a broad, mellow ridge with stunning views south toward the McCall Glacier and Old Snowy's pointed summit.

This next section is somewhat "airy" and can be intimidating; however, the trail is never as bad as it looks from a distance. It should be noted that many of these slopes can be snowbound well into July, and an ice axe and crampons may be required. That said, this is also the most stunning section of the hike because it travels along a jagged, narrow ridgeline.

The first exposed slope runs along a narrow footpath below Peak 7210's talus to a small, narrow saddle, where you can see Tieton Peak and Devils Horns due east of Old Snowy. From the saddle the trail seems to disappear, but a somewhat indiscernible path takes off to the right and quickly reveals itself through loose, broken rock as the main trail. Continue along the ridge until you reach a crest saddle on the south side of Old Snowy.

From here you have a couple of options. The PCT used to travel up and over the summit of Old Snowy (elevation 7,930 feet), and the remnants of the old trail are still visible from this location. The climber's trail ascends 0.6 miles and gains approximately 550 feet. If you still have the itch to explore, drop off the northern shoulder and switchback west to rejoin the PCT.

If the weather is bad or you have had enough excitement for one day, continue on the official PCT route that was blasted by the Forest Service in 1978. The route runs above the Packwood Glacier to the second-highest point on the PCT in Washington. Once again, the view is impressive. The emerald waters of Goat Lake, to the northwest, contrast strikingly with the deep reds, greens, and grays of the slopes surrounding it. Snap some photos and revel in the great scenery before retracing your steps back to camp.

DIRECTIONS From Packwood, drive east 19 miles on WA 12 to White Pass. Continue 7.5 miles and turn right on FR 1200 (a sign on the highway for Clear Lake marks the turn). Follow the paved road approximately 3 miles, and just as it begins to make a sharp curve, continue straight on FR 1207. Follow this dirt road another 5 miles or so to its end at the trailhead, where there is ample parking.

PERMIT Northwest Forest Pass required. Self-issued permits available at trailhead.

GPS Trailhead Coordinates	6 Old Snowy Mountain
UTM Zone (WGS 84)	10T
Easting	0625810
Northing	5159269
Latitude	N46.575198°
Longitude	W121.358118°

7 Round Mountain

SCENERY: ✿ ✿ ✿	HIKING TIME: *6–7 hours*
TRAIL CONDITION: ✿ ✿ ✿	GREEN TRAILS MAP: White Pass 303
CHILDREN: ✿ ✿	OUTSTANDING FEATURES: *Great views into*
DIFFICULTY: ✿ ✿ ✿	*Goat Rocks Wilderness, a somewhat "warm" alpine*
SOLITUDE: ✿ ✿ ✿ ✿	*lake to swim around in, and the chance to stand on*
DISTANCE: *12 miles*	*top of two different peaks*

A sign on popular White Pass reads RECREATION NEXT 23 MILES, *a dead giveaway as to the main attraction. It should, therefore, come as no surprise that the parking lot for the Pacific Crest Trail can be packed on any given weekend. Anglers, hunters, and hikers come from all around to explore the vast wilderness that surrounds this path. When I ventured on to the quiet, albeit steep, Twin Peaks Trail, I was more than pleasantly surprised not to see another soul on a warm, sunny Friday afternoon.*

🚶🚶 One of my favorite things is stumbling upon new areas right in my own backyard. I roped in a longtime local to do this hike with me, and as we laced our boots and stuffed our packs, I discovered that she had never hiked this trail. Easily bypassed by those wishing to remain on the PCT, this little side trail is a great place to avoid the crowds and take in some spectacular vistas.

From the parking area, head southbound on the PCT. The trail immediately crosses the south fork of Clear Creek, where a jaunt upstream eventually leads to Leech Lake. Conveniently located just north of Highway 12, the lake is a popular horse-camping destination and an access point for those traveling north on the PCT.

Continuing past the creek, the trail steadily climbs long, gradual switchbacks through stands of second-growth forests. At 1.3 miles the trail passes a small stream, whose waters flow into, instead of out of, Leech Lake. You walk only briefly along the stream bank before turning back into the cool shade of the forest. In another 0.5 miles,

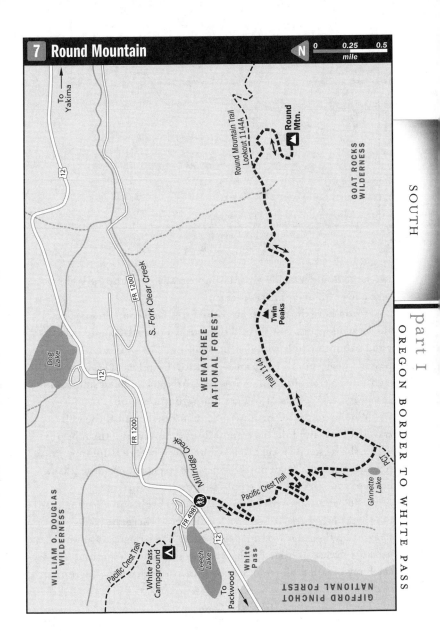

N
0   0.25   0.5
mile

To Yakima

12

FR 1200

S. Fork Clear Creek

Round Mountain Trail
Lookout 1144A

Round Mtn.

GOAT ROCKS
WILDERNESS

WENATCHEE
NATIONAL FOREST

Dog Lake

12

FR 1200

Twin Peaks

Trail 1144A

Millridge Creek

Pacific Crest Trail

Ginnette Lake

PCT

WILLIAM O. DOUGLAS
WILDERNESS

Pacific Crest Trail

White Pass
Campground

FR 498

Leech Lake

12

White Pass

To Packwood

GIFFORD PINCHOT
NATIONAL FOREST

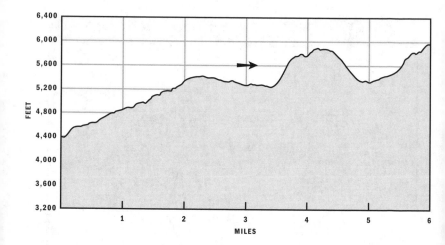

two large boulder fields provide ample seating for anyone wishing to take a load off and enjoy a little sun.

From here the trail reenters the forest and soon enters Goat Rocks Wilderness. Just beyond the sign, you pass Ginnette Lake, a good swimming hole with decent camping. The trail turns east and passes a boggy pond. Keep an eye out for Twin Peaks Trail 1144. The sign for the trail sits high up in a tree, on the left-hand side, and is somewhat easy to miss if you are not paying attention.

When you get to the junction, turn northeast off the well-traveled PCT and join the trail to Round Mountain, which begins with a short, steep descent to a lush meadow before flattening out as it wraps around a small point. Enjoy the level ground while it lasts because your first of a few climbs is about to begin.

The path to the first of the Twin Peaks begins on a mellow gradient that slowly works its way to a saddle. From here the trail shoots straight up the ridge, sending your heart rate straight up as well. I used the excuse of hiking with a local to stop every few minutes and catch my breath as she told me about the views that were beginning

Looking east from Round Mountain toward Clear and Rimrock lakes

to open on our ascent up the ridge. To the southwest lies Hogback Ridge, where you can see the PCT in the hillside just below the ridge as it continues south toward the heart of Goat Rocks Wilderness.

Resuming your climb, enjoy the multiplying views: the manicured runs of White Pass Ski Area to the west; the rugged, glaciated slopes of Old Snowy Mountain, Ives Peak, and Mount Curtis Gilbert to the southwest; and the craggy ridgelines of Bear Creek Mountain and Devils Horns to the south. The trail runs just below the peak's summit and descends through a steep, loose scree field to a prominent, windswept saddle. Dog Lake is to the north, at the base of Spiral Butte's conical slopes.

Spiral Butte and Dog Lake

From the saddle, the trail ascends through a stand of scraggly trees, crosses a small saddle, and switches to the north side of the ridge. It then travels below the second of the two peaks as it begins a 500-foot descent to a broad, forested saddle. The trail stays relatively level for 0.5 miles or so—a nice break from the ups and downs you've endured to this point. The uniformity of the woods is quickly interrupted by an entire hillside covered in small rocks and boulders. The trail makes a couple of small switchbacks along the flanks of the rocky slope before reentering the woods.

At 5.5 miles from the trailhead, you reach the turnoff for Round Mountain Lookout Trail 1144A. If you want to thru-hike, continue east another 2 miles to FR 840. It is approximately 14.7 miles from the PCT trailhead to the Round Mountain Trailhead via WA 12 and Tieton Road 1207. Continuing from the junction, head north up another series of switchbacks until you reach the abandoned fire lookout of Round Mountain, elevation 5,970 feet.

Forest Service employees stationed at the lookout (erected in the 1930s) monitored the area's frequent fires. The lookout was disassembled in 1976 when other methods of fire monitoring were established. Even without the lookout, the views from this perch make the climb well worth the effort. Mount Adams reveals itself for the first time to the south, and Clear and Rimrock lakes, to the east, twinkle in the afternoon light. Views to the north are somewhat obscured; however, a little maneuvering allows a glimpse of Mount Rainier. Tired and a little on the dusty side, you will want to take a dip in the refreshing waters of Ginnette Lake on the hike back out.

DIRECTIONS From Packwood follow WA 12 east 19 miles to White Pass. The trailhead is on the south side of the road, approximately 0.5 miles from White Pass Village.

PERMIT Northwest Forest Pass required.

GPS Trailhead Coordinates	7 Round Mountain
UTM Zone (WGS 84)	10T
Easting	0627767
Northing	5165868
Latitude	N46.634197
Longitude	W121.330763

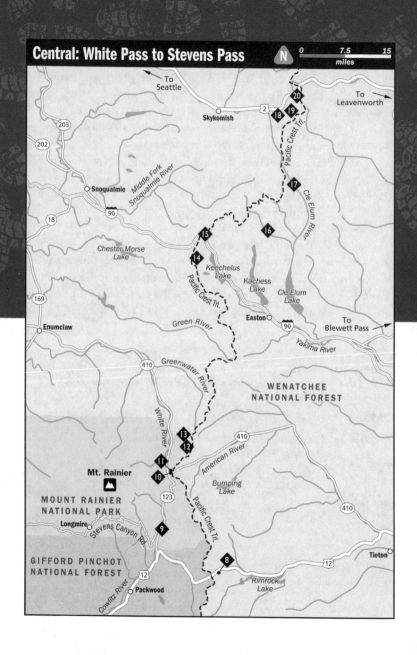

N

0   7.5   15
miles

To Seattle

2

Skykomish

203

202

18

90

Snoqualmie

Middle Fork Snoqualmie River

Pacific Crest Trl.

To Leavenworth

20

18   19

17

Cle Elum River

15

16

Chester Morse Lake

14

Keechelus Lake

Kachess Lake

Cle Elum Lake

169

Pacific Crest Trl.

Green River

Easton

90

To Blewett Pass

Yakima River

Enumclaw

410   Greenwater River

WENATCHEE NATIONAL FOREST

White River

13

410

12

American River

11

10

Mt. Rainier

MOUNT RAINIER NATIONAL PARK

123

Bumping Lake

410

Longmire

Stevens Canyon Rd.

9

Pacific Crest Trl.

Tieton

GIFFORD PINCHOT NATIONAL FOREST

8

Rimrock Lake

12

12

Cowlitz River

Packwood

2

CENTRAL

White Pass to Stevens Pass

8 Buesch and Dumbbell Lakes *(page 66)*

9 Laughingwater Creek *(page 73)*

10 Dewey Lake *(page 79)*

11 Sheep Lake and Sourdough Gap *(page 84)*

12 Bullion Basin to Silver Creek *(page 89)*

13 Big Crow Basin *(page 95)*

14 Mirror Lake *(page 101)*

15 Commonwealth Basin to Red Pass *(page 107)*

16 Spectacle Lake *(page 112)*

17 Cathedral and Deception Passes *(page 118)*

18 Surprise and Glacier Lakes *(page 125)*

19 Hope and Mig Lakes *(page 130)*

20 Chain and Doelle Lakes *(page 135)*

8 Buesch and Dumbbell Lakes

SCENERY: ✿ ✿ ✿	HIKING TIME: *1–2 days*
TRAIL CONDITION: ✿ ✿ ✿ ✿	GREEN TRAILS MAP: White Pass 303
CHILDREN: ✿ ✿ ✿	OUTSTANDING FEATURES: *A plethora of*
DIFFICULTY: ✿ ✿ ✿	*lakes to visit, an awesome location to take kids*
SOLITUDE: ✿ ✿ ✿	*camping for their first time, and moderate elevation*
DISTANCE: *16 miles*	*gain and loss*

One word of caution about this hike: bugs! While alpine lakes are the perfect place for us humans to hang out, the swampy marshlands and stagnant ponds that surround them provide the ideal environment for mosquitoes and other biting insects. If you can find the time in late summer or fall, save this hike for the off-season. Otherwise, make sure you bring plenty of mosquito netting and consider doing the loop in a moderately long day.

🚶🚶 There are two ways to begin this hike. The first option is to take off from the PCT trailhead, which is 0.5 miles northeast of White Pass on the north side of Highway 12. This trailhead is very popular with equestrians and can be packed on the weekend. A somewhat quieter option is to start from Dog Lake Campground, another 1.5 miles east past the turnoff for the PCT, on the north side of the road. There is only enough room for four vehicles, so if the parking spaces are taken, you might find yourself backtracking to the PCT trailhead.

Regardless of which trailhead you begin from, take a detailed map. There are a ton of options once you hit the northern lakes, and deciding which way to go can be a bit confusing. Whichever way you go, the terrain is anything but disappointing.

Leaving from Dog Lake Campground, follow the trailhead sign for Cramer Lake, and you soon reach the junction for Dark Meadow

8 Buesch and Dumbbell Lakes

N
0
0.5
1
mile
Tumac Mtn.
PCT
Trail 44
GIFFORD PINCHOT NATIONAL FOREST
Jess Lake
Pipe Lake
Benchmark Lake
Cowlitz Pass
Pillar Lake
Long John Lake
Trail 1142A
Buesch Lake
Dumbbell Lake
Trail 1142
Trail 56
Trail 1106
Trail 1106
Otter Lake
Cramer Mtn.
Trail 57
Pacific Crest Trail
Cramer Lake
Dancing Lady Lake
MT. BAKER-SNOQUALMIE NATIONAL FOREST
WILLIAM O. DOUGLAS WILDERNESS
Trail 60
Sand Lake
Dog Lake
Trail 1107
GOAT ROCKS WILDERNESS
12
Deer Lake
Pacific Crest Trail
FR 1200

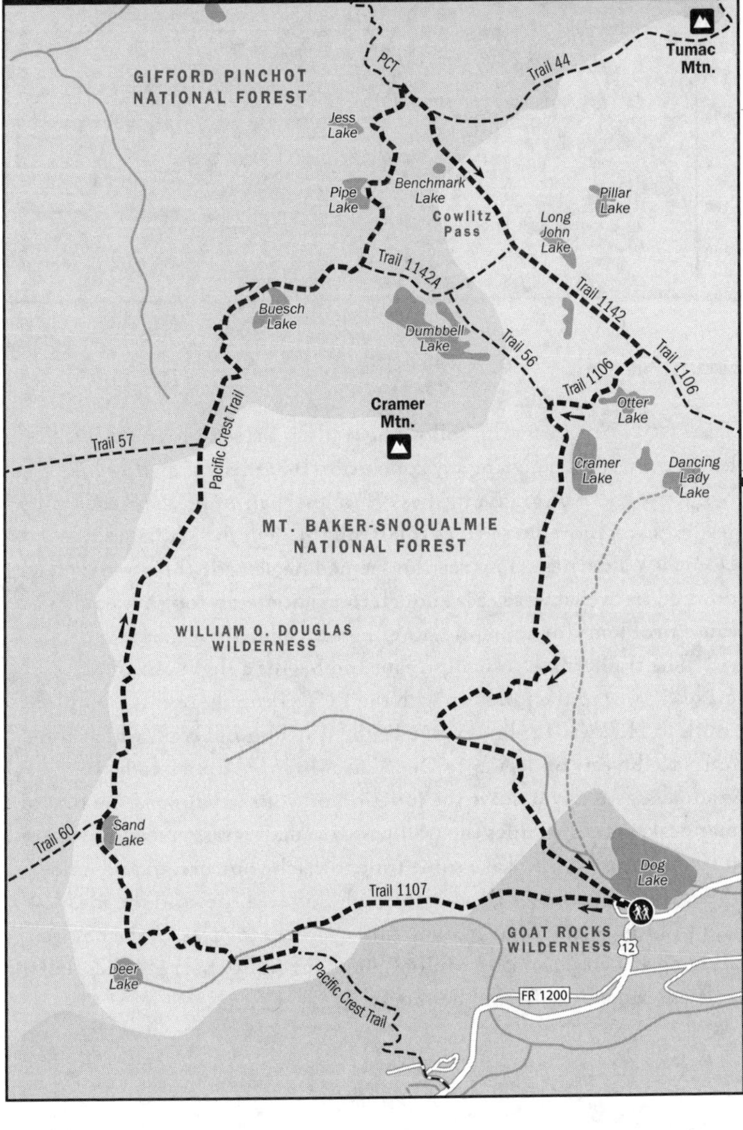

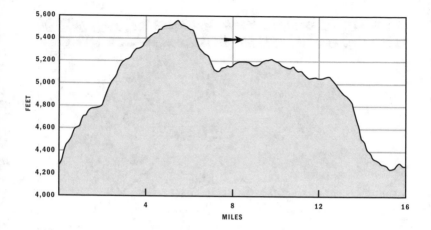

Trail 1107. Turn east and follow the trail up a steep incline that will leave you second-guessing my conclusion that this is a mellow hike. Not to worry: The gradient eases off in less than 1 mile, and the trail resumes an enjoyable pitch as you stroll through the William O. Douglas Wilderness. This section seemed neglected—there were a few downed trees that were easy enough to negotiate on foot but could cause problems for someone traveling with a horse or llama.

The trail crosses a small stream and begins a slight ascent as it makes its way to the junction with the PCT. From here it is 1.3 miles south to Highway 12; however, take the northbound trail, which contours to the east on its way to Deer Lake. Prepare for a steady, yet gradual ascent as you leave the junction on your way toward the first of many lakes. In 0.5 miles the trail passes a small, grassy meadow, where it levels out for a bit. Take some time to catch your breath and enjoy the sound of the water flowing through this area. Beyond the meadow you will follow and then cross an outlet stream for Deer Lake before arriving at a larger meadow full of low-lying huckleberry bushes, tall grasses, and alpine fir and hemlock.

Just as the trail begins to reenter the forest, you will notice a path that branches off to the south. This side trail will lead you to a camp at the southern end of Deer Lake. Proximity to Highway 12 makes this pretty little lake a very popular place to camp. Hitching posts and extremely large sites also reveal the amount of horse traffic this area sees. The lake is well liked for a reason, so if you happen to be here when no one is around, you may want to consider staying put for the night.

Continuing on the PCT, the trail contours north from the lake turnoff and follows a slight rise above the large meadow, where a small pond can be seen tucked among the tall, swaying grass. Soon you arrive at aptly named Sand Lake. The impact of campers at this well-liked campsite is less noticeable, and so are the people. A spur trail at the base of the lake's peninsula leads to a small shelter.

Just beyond the spur on the west side of the lake is a junction with Sand Lake Trail 60, which heads south 2.8 miles to FR 1284. The PCT continues north through an old burn, where grayish-black snags contrast strikingly with purple lupines and bright-green grasslands. In another mile or so, the trail passes a large boulder with a series of dinner plate–like rocks stacked neatly on top of it. As you round the corner, you get a good glimpse east toward Spiral Butte and Clear Lake.

The next few miles are fairly uninteresting; however, the easy walking makes the time go by fast. Just more than 6 miles along, the trail meets up with Cortright Creek Trail 57, a quiet, obscure route that takes you 4.5 miles west to FR 45. Remain heading north on the well-traveled PCT, where ponds, puddles, mud holes, and lakes continue to dominate the landscape. A small pass provides a change of scenery, as views open to the northwest, where Fryingpan Mountain rises above the forested ridgelines in the distance.

The trail remains relatively flat for the next mile or so. Two descending switchbacks lead you to the Buesch Lake basin, where you are first greeted with a scattering of small ponds in an expansive

CENTRAL

WHITE PASS TO STEVENS PASS

field of tall grass that shimmers in the wind. As you cross the outlet stream at 7.5 miles, you get a good view of the lake. The grassy shoreline makes it difficult to access the water, and better camping can be found farther down the line.

Head east from the lake and soon arrive at a junction. There are a couple of options from this point, but all of them eventually lead you back to where you started. Traveling east, in less than 0.5 miles you reach Dumbbell Lake, one of the larger bodies of water in this area. From there, head south toward Cramer Lake, and in about 5 miles you reach your starting point.

If you're feeling motivated, you can add a 2.5-mile mini-loop to your hike by continuing north on the PCT to Pipe Lake, whose northern shore boasts great camping. A short way north of the lake is Cowlitz Trail 44. Take this trail east, and in 0.2 miles you arrive at another decision-making point. Those of you who, like me, crave open, 360-degree views, should take the not-so-well-maintained but well-worth-the-effort Tumac Mountain Trail. Be prepared to sweat, though, because this little out-and-back adds another 3.4 miles and 1,100 feet of elevation gain.

Venturing on from the junction, Trail 1142 heads southeast and quickly comes to Benchmark Lake. This murky-looking pond has, for some reason, earned a name for itself—quite possibly because it lies just beyond a geological survey marker, which sits on a rock just off the trail. In another 0.5 miles, you reach the clear, lake-like waters of Long John Lake, whose grassy shores provide the perfect habitat for a wide range of birds. This spot is a bird lovers' paradise, and quiet campsites dot the area.

Just beyond the lake is Trail 1142A, which heads east to reach Dumbbell Lake in 0.7 miles. You can also continue southeast past, you guessed it, more puddles and ponds, to a junction that lies just beyond a section of trail that cuts through grassland. Turn off onto Cramer Lake Trail 1106 and head to the junction that takes you to

Layered rocks in the William O. Douglas Wilderness

Dumbbell Lake, as described above. Upon reaching the junction, turn south; the trail soon passes Cramer Lake. The route is a few hundred yards up from the lake; however, there are paths leading to good camping closer to the shoreline.

The next portion of trail remains in the forest, for the most part. A couple of open sections provide views of Spiral Butte's rocky west-facing slopes and Dog Lake's deep-blue waters, to the south. As you continue your descent, you can hear the grumble of the north fork of a creek that feeds into Dog Lake. This is your last major obstacle of the hike—there is no bridge at the crossing, so you'll have to wade through the cold water. Use caution: The rocks are extremely slippery even if the water is low. If you are at all concerned with water levels, it might be a good idea to do this hike in the opposite direction, in case high water requires you to turn around.

Bountiful berries

Less than 2 miles from the crossing is the junction with Dark Meadows Trail, which you started out on. It's just a few hundred yards to the trailhead and, yes, there is another lake for you to enjoy!

DIRECTIONS   From Packwood, head east on WA 12 to White Pass. Continue 2 miles east from the pass and turn left into Dog Lake Campground. Follow the one-way loop to the trailhead parking area.

PERMIT   Northwest Forest Pass required. Self-issued permits available at trailhead.

GPS Trailhead Coordinates	8 Buesch and Dumbbell Lakes
UTM Zone (WGS 84)	10T
Easting	0625413
Northing	5167844
Latitude	N46.652418°
Longitude	W121.360976°

9 Laughingwater Creek

SCENERY: ✿ ✿ ✿

TRAIL CONDITION: ✿ ✿ ✿ ✿

CHILDREN: ✿ ✿

DIFFICULTY: ✿ ✿ ✿

SOLITUDE: ✿ ✿ ✿ ✿

DISTANCE: *12–20 miles*

HIKING TIME: *1–2 days*

GREEN TRAILS MAPS: Mount Rainier East 270 *and* Bumping Lake 271

OUTSTANDING FEATURES: *Three Lakes, Two Lakes. Green lakes, blue lakes. What more could you want? How about stunning views of Mount Rainier, ample huckleberry picking, and excellent wildlife-viewing opportunities?*

When thinking of Mount Rainier National Park, most people simply envision the mountain, with its broken glaciers and rugged volcanic outcroppings. While the dramatic images are impressive, the park has a softer side that usually goes unnoticed. This is your chance to experience a place where mist rises from calm, clear lakes that lie in thick, old-growth forests; brightly colored dragonflies dance on the water's edge; and bull elk can be heard bugling during the rutting season on a crisp fall afternoon.

🚶🚶 One of the great things about this hike is that there are a few ways to do it. Depending on how much time, energy, and motivation you have, you can either hike the 6 miles into Three Lakes, have lunch, and head back out; pitch a tent at Three Lakes and do Two Lakes as a day hike; or take your time and spend a night at each lake. Note that Three Lakes is within the national park boundary, where firearms, pets, and campfires are prohibited. Also, if you decide to camp there, make sure to stop by any of the park's visitor information centers to obtain a backcountry permit.

To begin, head east, crossing Highway 123, to a small post that marks the trailhead for Laughingwater Creek. The trail starts off in an old-growth forest, where minute pinecones and thousands of needles cover the forest floor, creating a soft, cushy surface. In a little less than 1 mile, the trail gains a ridge and you can hear Laughingwater Creek giggling in a deep gorge far below. Follow the ridge proper a short distance before the trail drops then crests a forested plateau.

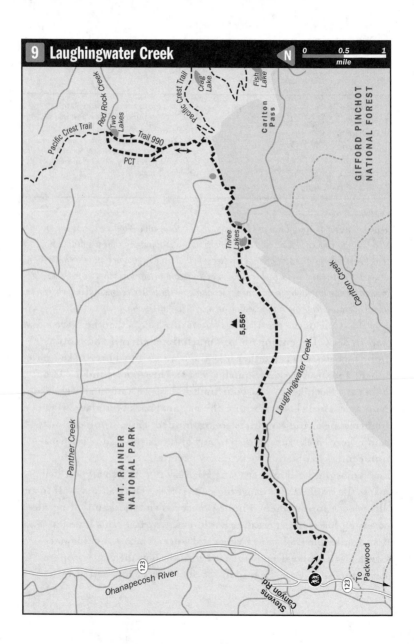

N

0   0.5   1
mile

Red Rock Creek

Pacific Crest Trail

Crag Lake

Fish Lake

Carlton Pass

GIFFORD PINCHOT
NATIONAL FOREST

Two Lakes

Trail 990

PCT

Three Lakes

Carlton Creek

5,556'

Laughingwater Creek

Panther Creek

MT. RAINIER
NATIONAL PARK

123

Ohanapecosh River

Stevens Canyon Rd.

To Packwood

123

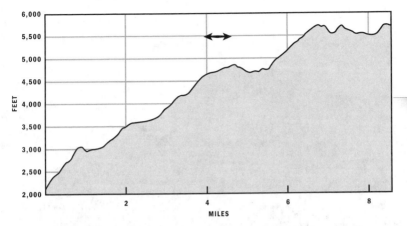

After enjoying level ground for a bit, you follow the trail down a few gentle switchbacks to a spot where you can see the creek for the first time. The path leaves the creek and soon passes a grassy pond, which you briefly glimpse through the thick vegetation before you resume your ever-steady climb toward Three Lakes.

In 1 mile or so the trail levels out and you find yourself walking beside the gentle waters of Laughingwater Creek. This pleasant section is filled with enormous Douglas firs and trickling feeder streams with wooden footbridges. As you wander along, take note of the huge rounds cut out of the trail by a hardworking trail crew. They make good seats, so consider taking a short break before beginning another fairly long uphill push.

From here the trail climbs away from the creek as it follows around the southeast side of point 5556. Along the way it crosses steep ravines and rocky creeks that plunge into the drainage below. The trail continues traveling through old-growth forests and occasionally crosses open slopes that allow for brief glimpses of the surrounding hillsides.

At approximately 5.5 miles, the trail tops out and enters the first of a series of lush meadows and reaches the former junction with the unmaintained, extremely hard to find East Boundary Trail. (Current

A stunning view of Mt. Rainier from the PCT

Green Trails maps no longer show it.) Continue on the main trail and begin a 0.5-mile descent to Three Lakes.

The first two lakes are tucked in next to each other and, at first glance, look as if they are one. As you wrap around the southernmost lake, you will notice a newly restored park service cabin, which houses backcountry rangers, trail crews, and other park service employees who work in the area. This camp is one of only four within the park that allows horses. There are two designated campsites and one group site uphill from the cabin.

The third and largest of the lakes is reached in another 0.2 miles. As you approach it, you leave the park and enter the William

O. Douglas Wilderness. Backcountry permits are not required here, so if the sites are full at the first two lakes, this is a feasible option. Whether or not you camp here, this lake has the best opportunities for swimming and should be explored.

Leaving the lake, the trail travels below a rocky knoll, giving it an alpine feel as it ascends toward the PCT. Soon you reenter the national park boundary. From the boundary line, the trail crosses a flat, grassy section before reentering the forest. A small pond tucked beside a stand of trees breaks up the monotony of the forest, as do the lupines that litter the forest floor.

In another mile the trail reaches a saddle with a small unnamed lake and your first opportunity for open views of Mount Rainier. Camping is prohibited at the lake; however, it is a great day-hike option from the Three Lakes camp if you don't feel like hiking all the way to Two Lakes. The trail ascends from the lake and, in 0.25 miles, reaches a creek that is dry and dusty by late summer. After a couple of switchbacks, the trail follows alongside the drainage then crosses the creek at its headwaters, which is nothing more than a concave meadow by the time summer rolls around.

In less than 0.25 miles you reach the junction with the PCT—and what a spectacular junction it is! Mount Rainier's crevasse-ridden glaciers dominate the foreground, almost making you overlook Mounts Adams and St. Helens towering proudly in the distance. The vistas are impressive from here on as you work your way onto a ridge, where you'll get a bird's-eye view of Bumping Lake to the northeast.

Just 0.3 miles from the junction with the PCT, you reach a large viewing area and an unmarked junction with Trail 990, which eventually leads you to Two Lakes. You can then make a small loop back to the PCT. Since the trail is tricky to find from this direction, continue on the PCT to the well-marked northern entrance and come back out on this trail.

Heading north on the PCT, the trail slips over to the east side of the divide, running below a ridgeline of short, stubby pillars of rock. After you crest the ridge, a decent-sized watering hole, aptly named One Lake, comes into view. This is a great spot to view wildlife, so if you have the time and the patience it may be worth hanging out here with a pair of binoculars on a lazy afternoon. Continuing on, the trail soon enters a small stand of trees and exits east through a bowl.

As the trail turns north again, keep an eye out for the Two Lakes junction. Once there, turn south and begin to descend the steep, rutted trail. Don't get discouraged: The trail quickly improves, and in 0.3 miles you reach the lake. There is excellent camping here, and permits are *not* required. To make the loop back to the PCT, continue around the western shore of the lake and follow the trail south. The path is easy to follow and in less than 1 mile you will be back at the large viewing area just off the PCT.

DIRECTIONS Follow WA 12 eastbound from Packwood and turn north onto WA 123. Continue past the Ohanapecosh Campground and visitor center, cross the Laughingwater Creek Bridge, and look for a pulloff on the west side of the road, about 0.1 mile from the bridge. (You may have to drive another 0.1 mile to the Stevens Canyon entrance to turn around.) Although you are within Mount Rainier National Park, you do not drive through an entrance station to access this particular trailhead and, therefore, do not have to pay the fee.

PERMIT Trailhead is outside of the park entrance fee station. Backcountry permit required at Three Lakes. Use designated sites. Make reservations or register in person at the Ohanapecosh Ranger Station during hours of operation.

GPS Trailhead Coordinates	9 Laughingwater Creek
UTM Zone (WGS 84)	10T
Easting	0610197
Northing	5178581
Latitude	N46.751681°
Longitude	W121.557194°

10 Dewey Lake

SCENERY: ☆☆☆☆
TRAIL CONDITION: ☆☆☆
CHILDREN: ☆☆☆☆
DIFFICULTY: ☆☆☆
SOLITUDE: ☆☆
DISTANCE: 8 miles (includes walking around lake)

HIKING TIME: 3–5 hours
GREEN TRAILS MAPS: Mount Rainier
East 270 and Bumping Lake 271
OUTSTANDING FEATURES: Alpine vistas in all
directions, great views of Mount Rainier, and abun-
dant camping along the peaceful shores of Dewey Lake

The trails leaving from Chinook Pass are usually packed with people on the weekends. An awe-inspiring drive, easy access to spectacular alpine scenery, and an entrance point to Mount Rainier National Park are the main draws, rain or shine. Do not be discour-aged by the crowds; there is enough amazing terrain for everyone to enjoy.

From the parking lot, head south to the trailhead, which is marked by a large interpretive sign that discusses the various trails in the area. Pick up the PCT just beyond this point and continue south 0.3 miles until you reach a junction. This hike can be done in either direction; however, I recommend starting out on the PCT for the grand views of Mount Rainier toward the end of the hike and good vistas of Dewey Lake before you descend to its shores.

If you decide to travel this way, continue east on the PCT across a wooden overpass that crosses Highway 410, marking the top of Chinook Pass at 5,400 feet and the boundary between Mount Rainier National Park and the Wenatchee National Forest. In 0.25 miles the trail enters the William O. Douglas Wilderness, an area named after Supreme Court Justice William O. Douglas, a Washington native who spent many of his summers exploring this vast area from the small mountain town of Goose Prairie.

Upon entering the wilderness, the trail travels southwest and skirts the northeast side of Naches Peak. A little less than 1 mile into the hike, the trail reaches a small tarn that sits among alpine benches. If

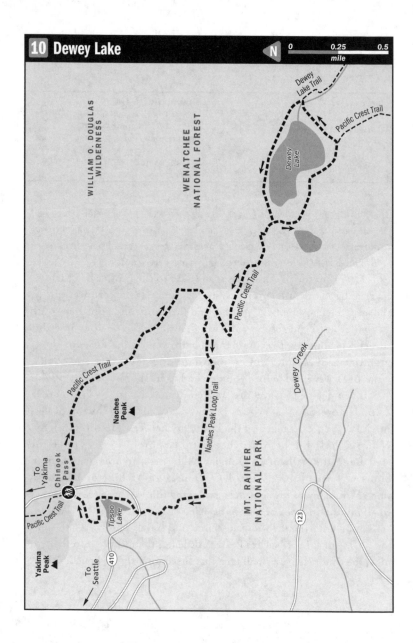

N

0   0.25   0.5
              mile

Dewey
Lake Trail

Pacific Crest Trail

WILLIAM O. DOUGLAS
WILDERNESS

WENATCHEE
NATIONAL FOREST

Dewey Lake

Pacific Crest Trail

Pacific Crest Trail

Naches Peak Loop Trail

Naches Peak ▲

Dewey Creek

To Yakima

Chinook Pass

Pacific Crest Trail

Tipsoo Lake

Yakima Peak ▲

To Seattle

410

MT. RAINIER
NATIONAL PARK

123

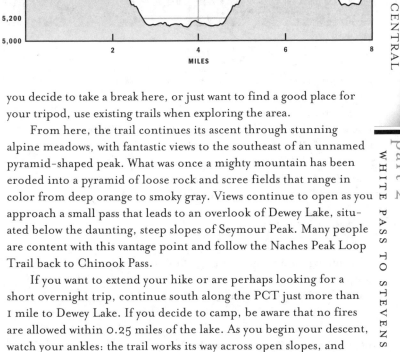

you decide to take a break here, or just want to find a good place for your tripod, use existing trails when exploring the area.

From here, the trail continues its ascent through stunning alpine meadows, with fantastic views to the southeast of an unnamed pyramid-shaped peak. What was once a mighty mountain has been eroded into a pyramid of loose rock and scree fields that range in color from deep orange to smoky gray. Views continue to open as you approach a small pass that leads to an overlook of Dewey Lake, situated below the daunting, steep slopes of Seymour Peak. Many people are content with this vantage point and follow the Naches Peak Loop Trail back to Chinook Pass.

If you want to extend your hike or are perhaps looking for a short overnight trip, continue south along the PCT just more than 1 mile to Dewey Lake. If you decide to camp, be aware that no fires are allowed within 0.25 miles of the lake. As you begin your descent, watch your ankles: the trail works its way across open slopes, and there is lots of loose rock scattered in the path. Soon the trail switchbacks to enter a thick, dark stand of trees. The view may not be the most exciting, but the trail evens out and turns into a pleasant stroll.

Alpine country surrounding Dewey Lake

At 2.7 miles the trail crosses several boardwalks that keep the path elevated above areas of fragile vegetation.

As you approach the lake, you pass a creek that leads to the small lake west of Dewey Lake. The lake itself is not too impressive; however, the wildflowers that surround it are worth checking out. Once you have taken your fair share of photos, continue along the PCT to reach the shores of Dewey Lake. The descent to the lake is well worth the extra effort, and those who simply enjoy its beauty from the viewpoint above miss out on the fields of wildflowers that surround the lake during peak season.

If you want more, check out the trail that circumnavigates the lake, adding 2 miles to the hike. Continue along the PCT 0.7 miles until you reach a junction where the PCT heads south to Anderson Lake. Take Dewey Way Trail 968A, and in 0.3 miles reach a bridge. Cross the bridge, and in few hundred feet you will see an unmaintained spur trail that heads around the north side of the lake 0.8 miles. Trail 968 descends into the American River drainage, which eventually rejoins Highway 410.

Once you have made the complete loop around the lake, continue back up the PCT to the junction with Naches Peak Loop Trail and follow it west toward Tipsoo Lake. Soon you will enter Mount Rainier National Park and get your first glimpse of Mt. Rainier itself. The views are impressive as the trail drops off a ridge and passes a small lake that sits among another great field of wildflowers. On a calm day, Rainier's Emmons Glacier is reflected in the still waters.

From here the terrain begins to change, with alpine meadows being replaced with stands of subalpine fir and mountain ash as you make your way down to Highway 410 and Tipsoo Lake. Use caution as you cross the busy road to reach the trailhead on the other side. Follow the trail around the shore of upper Tipsoo Lake in either direction until you arrive at a picnic area. Take an immediate right out of the picnic area and ascend quickly above the lakes into a thick stand of trees that top out in a small, open meadow. Just on the other side of the meadow you will reach the Highway 410 overpass and the end of the loop. Head north on the PCT back to the parking lot.

DIRECTIONS FROM SEATTLE: Take I-5 to I-405 and head east. Continue on I-405 to WA 167 and head south to WA 410. Follow WA 410 east to the small town of Greenwater. From here, WA 410 heads south to Mount Rainier National Park. Enter the park. Just before WA 410 meets up with WA 123, WA 410 turns east up to Chinook Pass. Drive to Chinook Pass and park in the large lot on the west side of the road.

FROM TACOMA: Drive east on WA 512 to WA 167 and head north. Follow the directions above to reach Chinook Pass.

FROM YAKIMA: Drive west on US 12 to WA 410. Head west on WA 410 to Chinook Pass. Park in the large lot on the west side of the road.

PERMIT Northwest Forest Pass required. Self-issued permit available at trailhead.

GPS Trailhead Coordinates	10 Dewey Lake
UTM Zone (WGS 84)	10T
Easting	0612932
Northing	5192308
Latitude	N46.874713°
Longitude	W121.518009°

11 Sheep Lake and Sourdough Gap

SCENERY: ✿ ✿ ✿ ✿

TRAIL CONDITION: ✿ ✿ ✿ ✿ ✿

CHILDREN: ✿ ✿ ✿ ✿ ✿

DIFFICULTY: ✿ ✿

SOLITUDE: ✿ ✿

DISTANCE: 6.4 miles round-trip to Sourdough Gap

HIKING TIME: 3–5 hours

GREEN TRAILS MAPS: Mount Rainier East 270 and Bumping Lake 271

OUTSTANDING FEATURES: Alpine lake, fields of colorful wildflowers in late July and August, short easy hike for kids, and dramatic glimpses of Mount Rainier near Sourdough Gap

This popular trail from Chinook Pass heads north from the same trailhead parking lot as the Dewey Lake hike. This is a great introductory backpack for children or anyone else who is looking to "get their feet wet." If you plan to camp here, be aware that Sheep Lake sits at 5,800 feet, so nights can be chilly, no matter what time of year it is.

🚶🚶 From the parking lot, head north along the PCT. From the moment your feet hit the trail, you are immersed in fields of wildflowers—beargrass, scarlet paintbrush, and columbine, to name just a few. The trail parallels the highway for the first mile; however, the colorful hillside distracts you from the traffic below. At 1.3 miles the trail turns north and enters the cool shade of the forest, while the highway begins its eastern descent toward Pleasant Valley. From here, the trail meanders through alpine fir trees and meadows of lupine as it gains the last 300 feet to Sheep Lake.

The trail tops out along the lake's southern shores. A flat, sandy spot among large boulders is a great place to have lunch or take a nap in the afternoon sun. This spot is extremely popular on weekends or sunny, warm weekdays, so plan to share your break with others. The lake is the perfect place to take kids on a short overnight backpacking trip, and there is a good chance that they will have other kids to run around and explore with. If you decide to take some time and enjoy the alpine beauty, please help protect this fragile area by using some basic Leave No Trace principles; take breaks in areas that have already

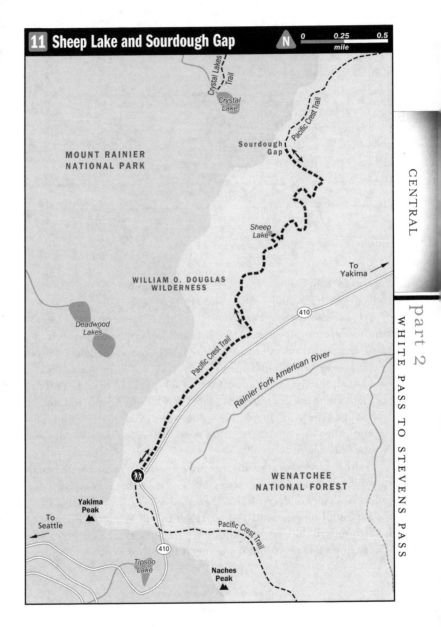

Crystal Lakes Trail

Crystal Lake

Pacific Crest Trail

Sourdough Gap

MOUNT RAINIER
NATIONAL PARK

Sheep Lake

To Yakima

WILLIAM O. DOUGLAS
WILDERNESS

410

Deadwood Lakes

Pacific Crest Trail

Rainier Fork American River

WENATCHEE
NATIONAL FOREST

Yakima Peak

To Seattle

410

Pacific Crest Trail

Tipsoo Lake

Naches Peak

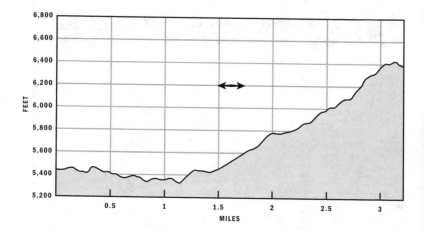

been used, camp at least 100 feet from the lake, and use existing trails to get water, find a camp, and explore the shoreline.

If you are revitalized and want more after your stint at the lake, continue around its eastern shoreline and head up to Sourdough Gap. The trail climbs steeply from the lake but soon mellows out as it snakes its way through open meadows. At 2.5 miles you enter a stand of alpine firs where a small U-shaped spur trail branches off to the right and provides your first glimpse of Mount Adams and the snowcapped peaks of Goat Rocks Wilderness. Don't worry if you miss the trail; the views open up in 0.25 miles, affording vistas of Mount Adams once again.

While the views in the distance are impressive, those immediately in front of you are just as noteworthy. The ridgeline is composed of pillars in shades of deep black and gray, which contrast sharply with the surrounding greenery. The trail rises to run below the ridge as it heads toward the pass. Just after the 3-mile mark, the trail crosses a scree slope that pours out from one of the columns above. Almost

Mt. Rainier from Sourdough Gap

immediately after you cross this slope you catch a quick glimpse of Mount Rainier through a gap in the ridgeline to the west. Pay close attention because the view is brief and easy to miss.

You reach Sourdough Gap at 3.2 miles. There are a couple of options from this point, the first a short jaunt over to the Mount Rainier National Park boundary. (If you decide to enter the park boundary, be aware that pets or firearms are prohibited.) Continue north from the gap and you will soon come to a junction; continue north across a scree slope to a small pass. Beyond the pass, you quickly reach the park boundary and, begin a steep descent along an unmaintained trail to the aptly named Crystal Lake. For those hikers looking for a less adventurous outing, there is a small knoll just below the pass that has stunning views of Mount Rainier. Make sure to bring your camera to appreciate this photographers' playground.

If you want to do a long hike with a couple of friends, the second option is a thru-hike to the Crystal Mountain Ski Area. From the gap, continue northeast along the PCT to Bear Gap (3.3 miles). From here, follow the directions from Bear Gap in the description for Bullion Basin to Silver Creek (the total hike is approximately 9 miles from Chinook Pass).

DIRECTIONS   FROM SEATTLE: Take I-5 to I-405 and head east. Continue on I-405 to WA 167 and head south to WA 410. Follow WA 410 east to the small town of Greenwater. From here, WA 410 heads south to Mount Rainier National Park. Drive through the entrance. Just before WA 410 meets up with WA 123, 410 turns east up to Chinook Pass. Drive to Chinook Pass and park in the large lot on the west side of the road.

FROM TACOMA: Drive east on WA 512 to WA 167 and head north. Follow the directions above to reach Chinook Pass.

FROM YAKIMA: Drive west on US 12 to WA 410. Head west on WA 410 to Chinook Pass. Park in the large lot on the west side of the road.

PERMIT   Northwest Forest Pass required. Backcountry permit is required at Crystal Lake. Make reservations or register in person at the White River Ranger Station during hours of operation. Self-issued permit available at trailhead for Sheep Lake.

GPS Trailhead Coordinates	11 Sheep Lake and Sourdough Gap
UTM Zone (WGS 84)	10T
Easting	0612920
Northing	5192472
Latitude	N46.876194°
Longitude	W121.518125°

12 Bullion Basin to Silver Creek

SCENERY: ✿ ✿ ✿ ✿ ✿
TRAIL CONDITION: ✿ ✿ ✿
CHILDREN: ✿ ✿
DIFFICULTY: ✿ ✿ ✿ ✿
SOLITUDE: ✿ ✿ ✿ ✿
DISTANCE: *7 miles*

HIKING TIME: *3–4 hours*
GREEN TRAILS MAP: Mount Rainier East 270
OUTSTANDING FEATURES: *Solitude, exceptional views of Mount Rainier, and myriad trails to keep you busy for as long as you like*

I tend to avoid weekend crowds whenever possible. However, there are times when getting out on a weekday just isn't possible, which is why I was so excited to find this relatively unknown loop. The scenery is breathtaking, the trails are quiet, and the hiking options are endless. Make sure you bring a map. Even the most experienced hikers are bound to make a wrong turn at one of the many junctions without one.

🚶 This trail begins with a somewhat exciting 2.2-mile drive up a steep, rocky Forest Service road that leaves you wondering, "Am I going the right way?" When you finally reach the trailhead, your only indicators are a couple of Forest Service trail signs and a small pullout on the side of the road where only about four cars can squeeze in.

From the pullout on FR 410, head toward Bullion Basin Trail 1156 and take note of Silver Creek Trail 1192, your exit route on your right. The trail heading toward Bullion Basin is steep and dusty for the first 0.25 miles—a sign of the horsepackers who frequent this section—and crosses the road a couple of times before arriving at a clearing that looks out toward the ski area.

After a couple of switchbacks, the trail makes its way up the creek, and at 0.6 miles a spur trail leads down to the water. This is a good spot to let thirsty dogs grab a drink before continuing up the trail; there is no more easily accessible water until you reach the basin.

At 1 mile the real beauty of this hike begins as the trail alternates between lush meadows and mature, healthy stands of fir and hemlock.

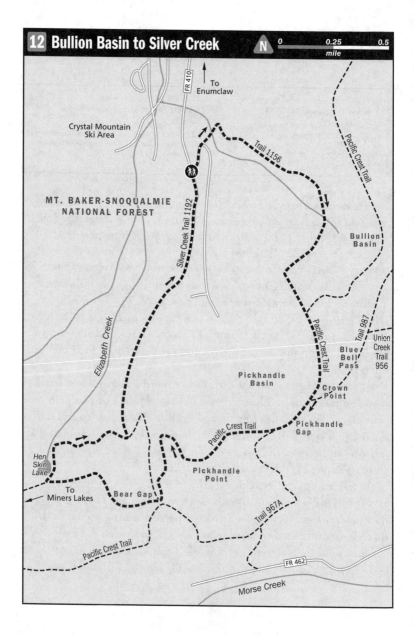

N

0   0.25   0.5
mile

To
Enumclaw

Crystal Mountain
Ski Area

FR 410

Trail 1156

Pacific Crest Trail

MT. BAKER-SNOQUALMIE
NATIONAL FOREST

Silver Creek Trail 1192

Bullion
Basin

Trail 987

Union
Creek
Trail
956

Elizabeth Creek

Pacific Crest Trail

Blue
Bell
Pass

Pickhandle
Basin

Crown
Point

Pickhandle
Gap

Pacific Crest Trail

Pickhandle
Point

Hen
Skin
Lake

To
Miners Lakes

Bear Gap

Trail 967A

Pacific Crest Trail

FR 462

Morse Creek

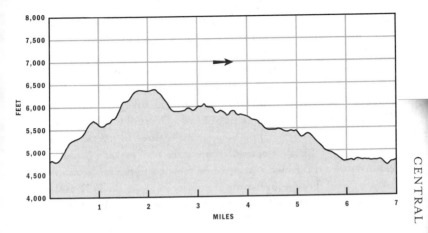

At 1.2 miles the trail opens up and Mount Rainier can be seen to the southwest, providing a stunning backdrop to the slopes of the ski area. In 0.25 miles you reach Bullion Basin, a large meadow with meandering streams that weave through the tall grass. As you enter the meadow, notice a steep, rugged path to the east that heads out of the basin and up toward the ridge to the PCT. To help prevent erosion, continue on the mail trail the short distance to Blue Bell Pass and the intersection with the PCT. Once you have crossed the meadow you pass a large campsite with a couple of hitching posts. If you plan to camp here, be prepared to share with horses.

Just past the campsite, cross the creek as the trail climbs out of the basin to head south. At 1.8 miles is the first of three steep switchbacks that round the shoulder of the ridge. It may feel as if you are topping out at a pass, but you still have 0.4 miles to go. This is, however, a fantastic location to stop for lunch or a light snack. Rainier dominates the skyline and steep slopes of subalpine daisies and lupine extend from the ridge into the valley below. After a short break, continue climbing on the west side of the ridge as you make your way toward the PCT. To the north, the PCT teeters along the ridgeline en route to Scout Pass and Norse Peak, a great out-and-back hike.

For those interested in continuing, head south on the PCT. In a few hundred feet you reach Blue Bell Pass (6,300 feet), which sits between Summit 6479 and Crown Point. The hike from the pass to Crown Point is not for the faint of heart. The trail is narrow and exposed, with steep, sweeping views in every direction. As you round Crown Point, the angle eases off a bit as the trail makes a gradual eastern descent through a large, open meadow to the junction with Union Creek Trail 956. Continue southwest along the PCT as the trail makes one large switchback to Pickhandle Gap and the William O. Douglas Wilderness boundary.

At 3.2 miles you reach the gap and yet another junction, this time with Trail 967A. The trail makes a stout ascent from Morse Creek, so don't be surprised to find fellow hikers out of breath and taking a well-earned break. From the gap, the trail rises slightly as it heads around Pickhandle Point. In 0.7 miles the trail makes a long switchback to the south as it crosses a ridge and heads to the five-way junction of Bear Gap (5,880 feet).

Even for the most experienced hikers, this is a confusing junction. Many of the signs are worn and lack maps. There are two options for getting back to FR 410: The first is to head north, traveling below the trail you just came in on; the second is to head west to Hen Skin Lake, which adds an extra mile or so to the hike but is more interesting.

If you decide to go to the lake, take the left of the two branches as you stand looking north from the junction. The trail gradually passes through stands of forest and open meadows and arrives at the lake 0.7 miles from the gap. As the trail makes a final switchback toward the shoreline, you reach the junction to Miners Lakes, two smaller lakes just to the west of Hen Skin. Continue around the lake's

Approaching Blue Bell Pass

perimeter to the outlet, where the trail reaches an unmarked junction. Stay to the right and descend to Jim Town, an old mining camp next to Elizabeth Creek.

This final junction of the hike is relatively straightforward. Follow the signs for Silver Creek Trail 1192, which follows Elizabeth Creek briefly before it rapidly drops away. The trail is fairly unremarkable until you pass a small tributary on a footbridge next to an old mine. Shortly after this, you travel beneath a ski lift and come out on a road that takes you back to FR 410.

DIRECTIONS From Enumclaw head east on WA 410 and, in approximately 34 miles, turn left at the sign for Crystal Mountain Ski Area onto Crystal Mountain Road (FR 7190). Continue up the road 4.2 miles and turn left onto FR 410 (not to be confused with WA 410), marked by a brown, metal sign. Use caution when driving up the road; it is narrow and steep in places and occasionally requires backing up if another car comes in the opposite direction. Follow the road 2.2 miles and park in the small pullout on the right side, just before the road begins to switchback.

PERMIT Northwest Forest Pass required.

GPS Trailhead Coordinates	12 Bullion Basin to Silver Creek
UTM Zone (WGS 84)	10T
Easting	0616527
Northing	5199366
Latitude	N46.937586°
Longitude	W121.469030°

13 Big Crow Basin

SCENERY: ✿ ✿ ✿ ✿
TRAIL CONDITION: ✿ ✿ ✿
CHILDREN: ✿ ✿
DIFFICULTY: ✿ ✿ ✿ ✿
SOLITUDE: ✿ ✿ ✿
DISTANCE: *12.5 miles*

HIKING TIME: *6–8 hours or overnight*
GREEN TRAILS MAP: Mount Rainier East 270
OUTSTANDING FEATURES: *Open meadows, a rickety old shelter, expansive views of numerous peaks, and a chance to glimpse mountain goats roaming the hills*

This loop hike explores the amazing subalpine terrain just north of Crystal Mountain Ski Area. While your jaunt on the PCT is a mere mile, the surrounding terrain is stunning. Make sure to bring plenty of water: Sources are limited and the trail can be hot and dry on a midsummer day.

🚶🚶 From the trailhead, you immediately begin a steep, dusty hike up a series of relentless switchbacks. The occasional flutter of a flushed grouse and the cool shade of a silver fir forest make this section somewhat enjoyable, despite your having to trudge a consistent uphill grade. In just under 1 mile, the trail arrives at the old Norse Peak trail, which is now closed to restore areas that have been damaged by erosion. As you resume your hike along the main trail, you can see where people have cut switchbacks, eroding sections of the new trail. Please stay on the main path and resist taking shortcuts—they will abbreviate your hike by only a few seconds anyway.

As you continue to climb, the trail switchbacks a few more times before paralleling a drainage where you can occasionally catch glimpses south toward Crystal Mountain Ski Area. At 1.9 miles the trail breaks out of the forest, and you can see the tip-top of Mount Rainier behind the ridgelines that spread from the summit of Crystal Mountain. This view is a teaser for what is to come.

The trail winds through open fields interspersed with small stands of evergreens for the next 0.5 miles before arriving at the

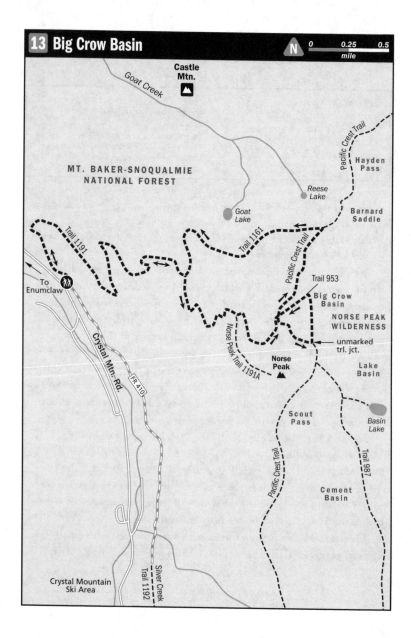

N

0   0.25   0.5
mile

Goat Creek

Castle Mtn. ▲

MT. BAKER-SNOQUALMIE
NATIONAL FOREST

Reese Lake

Goat Lake

Pacific Crest Trail

Hayden Pass

Barnard Saddle

Trail 1191

Trail 1161

Pacific Crest Trail

Trail 953

Big Crow Basin

To Enumclaw

NORSE PEAK
WILDERNESS

unmarked trl. jct.

Lake Basin

Crystal Mtn. Rd.

Norse Peak Trail 1191A

Norse Peak ▲

Basin Lake

FR 410

Scout Pass

Trail 987

Pacific Crest Trail

Cement Basin

Crystal Mountain
Ski Area

Silver Creek Trail 1192

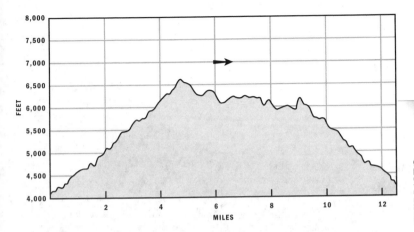

junction for Goat Lake. Take note of this location—it is where you will exit if you are interested in doing this hike as a loop. Remain on Trail 1191 as it makes one last, good uphill push. Rainier displays itself in all its glory 1 mile or so from the junction, allowing you to take a breather and enjoy the view.

Just a bit farther you reach a narrow ridge that is forested on one side and open on the other. As you ascend, keep an eye out for an unmarked spur trail that branches to the left and descends into Big Crow Basin. The trail along the ridgeline eventually leads you to the summit of Norse Peak, elevation 6,856 feet, and the site of an old fire lookout erected in the 1930s and removed in 1956. Not much remains of the lookout; however, if you're feeling strong, the views are well worth the extra 1.4 miles.

If you're not feeling the call to summit Norse Peak, the wild-flowers in the bowl below are just as stunning. The trail descends the ridge through a steep, loose section that mellows as you work around the upper part of the basin. Fields of flowers, including columbine, tiger lilies, valerian, and asters, hold your interest, and in less than 1 mile you will be on the PCT.

Looking down toward Basin Lake

From here you have a couple of options. Those of you looking to get out overnight should head south on the PCT to a junction with Basin Lake Trail 987. The lake itself is less than 1 mile from the junction; however, it loses 600 feet in elevation, making it somewhat of a bear to climb back out of. That said, the stunning turquoise waters in the shadow of a behemoth rock outcropping provide the ideal backcountry campsite and quickly make you forget the hike that awaits you in the morning.

If you are looking for something a little less ambitious, you can head east 0.25 miles on Crow Lake Way Trail 953. This short excursion brings you to an old, weathered shelter built by the Civilian Conservation Corps in the 1930s. While the structure's saggy frame and perforated roof may not provide much shelter these days, its location at the edge of Big Crow Basin's expansive meadow makes it anything but disappointing. There is a small stream nearby that trickles year-round.

While exploring the area around the shelter, you may encounter a well-used path that takes off behind the hitching post and eventually leads you back to the PCT, but it is steep, and having to negotiate the loose rock means you won't save much time. To help prevent further erosion, retrace your steps on Trail 953.

Once you arrive back at the junction, head north on the PCT. The trail traverses a bowl, and in 0.5 miles reaches Barnard Saddle. Continue along the ridge, and when you enter a stand of dense trees, keep an eye out for a signed junction to Cement Basin and take the unmarked trail that travels west toward Goat Lake. In less than 1 mile, you enter a spectacular basin where eroding pinnacles leave behind fields of talus slopes strewn with mountain goat paths. If you're lucky, you may see these impressive animals weaving their way through the cliff bands above.

As you work your way across the bottom of the talus field, Goat Lake slowly comes into view. The trail travels well above the lake (which resembles more of a large pond); however, there is a series of game trails that work their way down to the water's edge. More impressive than the lake itself is its backdrop, Castle Rock. This broad, massive rock formation across the valley rises sharply and will have you stumbling in your tracks.

From the basin the trail ascends to a saddle, then climbs directly up a ridge to three hitching posts. As you gain the ridge, look for a trail off to the west that turns sharply south. This trail takes you back to Trail 1191, which is unmarked and easy to miss if you are not paying attention. If you reach the hitching posts, you have gone too far. As you descend, Rainier greets you once again and the trail you came up on can be seen through gaps in the trees. You soon arrive back at Trail 1191, and in 2.5 miles you are back at the trailhead. The small town of Greenwater is a short drive from the parking area and is the ticket for refueling a tired body.

DIRECTIONS From Enumclaw head east on WA 410 and, in about 34 miles, turn left at the sign for Crystal Mountain Ski Area onto Crystal Mountain Road (FR 7190). Continue up the road 4.2 miles and turn left onto FR 410 (not to be confused with WA 410), which is marked by a brown, metal sign. The best place to park is at the large pullout at the beginning of the road. Walk 0.25 miles up FR 410 to the trailhead for Norse Peak, on the left side of the road.

PERMIT Northwest Forest Pass required.

GPS Trailhead Coordinates	13 Big Crow Basin
UTM Zone (WGS 84)	10T
Easting	0615620
Northing	5202073
Latitude	N46.962095°
Longitude	W121.480253°

14 Mirror Lake

SCENERY: 🌲 🌲 🌲	HIKING TIME: *4–5 hours*
TRAIL CONDITION: 🌲 🌲 🌲 🌲	GREEN TRAILS MAP: Snoqualmie Pass 207
CHILDREN: 🌲 🌲 🌲 🌲	OUTSTANDING FEATURES: *A gorgeous alpine*
DIFFICULTY: 🌲 🌲	*lake that reflects Tinkham Peak's craggy outline, a*
SOLITUDE: 🌲 🌲	*couple of peaks for summit-hungry folks to scramble*
DISTANCE: 6 miles	*up, and a good day hike or overnight trip for kids*

There is an abundance of hiking options along this corridor, mainly because of the extensive logging-road system that surrounds it. Mirror Lake, for example, can be approached on the PCT from the north or the south. Although the southern approach is shorter, the trail lies in a clear-cut, and you end up spending more time in the car than out in the woods. To ensure you make the most of your visit, I have listed a few hiking alternatives.

🚶 This hike is a true Washington treasure. Surrounded by a patchwork of logged slopes, the trail lies within the protective boundaries of an area that the Forest Service obtained in 2000 in hopes of preserving and rehabilitating a healthy forest along the Central Cascade crest.

To begin, head south on the PCT through an old clear-cut that immediately reminds you how fortunate we are that this area has been saved. For the first 0.25 miles, the trail is devoid of trees but thick with huckleberry bushes. It isn't uncommon to see a few people in the field in late summer or early fall with buckets in their hands and purplish-blue stains on their lips. Beyond the opening, the trail enters a thriving forest and crosses a few trickling creeks. Within the first mile, views open to the east, toward the deep-blue waters of the large Keechelus Lake and the fairly murky waters of the much smaller Twin Lakes.

In 0.5 miles, the trail enters a meadow at the base of Silver Peak, a popular springtime scramble that can be approached from the PCT via Olallie Meadow or from the more standard route along the ridgelines

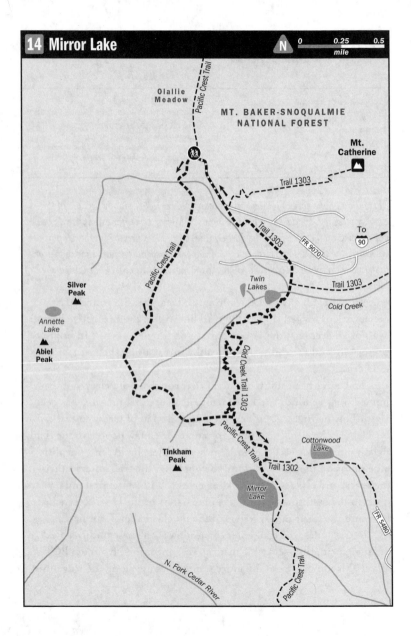

N

0   0.25   0.5
mile

Olallie
Meadow

Pacific Crest Trail

MT. BAKER-SNOQUALMIE
NATIONAL FOREST

**Mt.
Catherine**

Trail 1303

Trail 1303

FR 9070

To
90

Trail 1303

Cold Creek

**Silver
Peak**

Pacific Crest Trail

Twin
Lakes

Annette
Lake

**Abiel
Peak**

Cold Creek Trail 1303

**Tinkham
Peak**

Cottonwood
Lake

Pacific Crest Trail

Trail 1302

Mirror
Lake

FR 5480

N. Fork Cedar River

Pacific Crest Trail

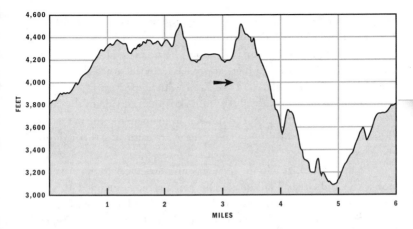

that fall toward Annette Lake on the peak's western side. Continuing along the trail, you reach Tinkham Peak, another popular scramble, southeast of Silver. Ambitious hikers have been known to tackle Tinkham, Silver, and Abiel (directly south of Silver) in a single day.

Remaining on the well-maintained trail, descend a couple of switchbacks, cross a small boulder field, and make a short climb to a bench near some watering holes. The trail can be mucky through this section, but the view of Tinkham should distract you from the suctioning sound your boots are making. From here the trail continues its ever-gradual ascent across a mixture of forested slopes and open hillsides to arrive at a broad pass in 2.8 miles.

To make a loop out of this hike, head down Cold Creek Trail 1303 toward Twin Lakes. Before doing so, however, descend a quick 0.5 miles to Mirror Lake along the PCT.

From the saddle, the Mirror Lake trail winds down a couple switchbacks, losing 300 feet in 0.5 miles, with views of Cottonwood Lake to the east (left). Like most of the lakes in this area, Cottonwood has a much shorter approach via a 1.1-mile excursion on Trail 1302 (leaving from FR 5480). The PCT intersects this trail just before you

CENTRAL

part 2
WHITE PASS TO STEVENS PASS

reach Mirror Lake, so if you're feeling energetic you can add 1 mile by hiking out and back to Cottonwood.

As you approach Mirror Lake, don't be surprised by the crowds along its shoreline. Many hikers approach it on the much shorter (and less interesting) Mirror Lake Trail, which joins the PCT as it approaches from the south. Both trails skirt the east side of the lake, where Tinkham's reflection can be seen in the placid, blue water. For those interested in sleeping outside, there are campsites throughout the area.

To make this hike a loop, reverse your course back to the junction with Cold Creek Trail 1303. This route is recommended only for experienced hikers and should not be attempted with children. The trail to Twin Lakes is steep (losing 1,400 feet in 1.7 miles), brushy, and can be slick as slime if there is any moisture in the air. On a positive note, you're almost guaranteed solitude all the way to the lake.

As you leave the saddle, the trail descends tight switchbacks on a somewhat slanted trail, where roots conspire to trip you. In 1 mile the trail crosses a large boulder field lined with devil's club, alders, and brambles. As you reach the valley floor, the trail skirts the south side of the lake, passing through a section of head-high brush to eventually spit you out at the outlet. Cross the notched log to access the lake's peaceful shores.

You may notice a faint footpath that cuts through the tall grass and marshy meadows and travels around most of the lake. Exploring the area, you may have trouble finding the second of the Twin Lakes: It's not you . . . the second lake has shrunk over time and resembles more of a large meadow these days.

Back on the trail, you pass a couple of nice campsites along a creek that drains from the lake. The trail soon joins Mount Catherine Trail 1348. From here Cold Creek Trail, which you were on, heads east to end 0.8 miles ahead, at FR 9070. If you're tired of traveling on rugged trails, take this trail to the road and walk back to your car at Windy

Mirror Lake lies in the shadow of Tinkham Peak.

Pass. This option adds a couple miles to your hike and gains about the same elevation as the Mount Catherine Trail.

If you're ready to get the hike over with, continue on the rarely frequented Mount Catherine Trail. The trail soon crosses a Forest Service road. Do not confuse this with FR 9070, and make sure you pick up the trail on the far side of the road. From here the trail climbs steeply along the east side of a brushy creek. The trail is overgrown and mucky in places, but the going is easier than on Cold Creek. Six hundred feet farther (approximately 1 mile from Twin Lake), you reach FR 9070, at an obscure, unmarked trailhead. Turn left and head uphill 0.25 miles back to your car. The total loop distance is 7 miles, not including the side trip to Mirror Lake.

DIRECTIONS Drive I-90 to Snoqualmie Pass and get off at Hyak, Exit 54. Follow signs to Hyak Ski Area. Go straight through a double stop sign (that's right, two stop signs). Before you reach the ski area parking lot, follow Hyak Drive as it curves left, back toward the interstate. The road quickly veers right and continues through a housing development. Ignore the dead-end sign and continue driving, entering a gate and passing a sewage-treatment plant, on the left side of the road (at 0.5 miles). Just beyond, the road becomes gravel. You are now on FR 9070.

In 2 miles, the trail passes the Cold Creek Trailhead (barely visible from the road) at a hairpin turn. Continue driving to an obvious clear-cut and you'll soon reach Windy Pass. Keep an eye out for the Mirror Lake/PCT trailhead on the left (south) side of the road (5 miles from the double stop sign). Drive slowly and watch for cyclists in this designated mountain-biking area.

PERMIT Northwest Forest Pass required.

GPS Trailhead Coordinates	14 Mirror Lake
UTM Zone (WGS 84)	10T
Easting	0617247
Northing	5247802
Latitude	N47.373153°
Longitude	W121.446932°

15 Commonwealth Basin to Red Pass

SCENERY: ✿ ✿ ✿ ✿	DISTANCE: *10 miles*
TRAIL CONDITION: ✿ ✿ ✿ ✿	HIKING TIME: *5 hours*
CHILDREN: ✿ ✿ ✿ ✿	GREEN TRAILS MAP: Snoqualmie Pass 207
DIFFICULTY: ✿ ✿ ✿	OUTSTANDING FEATURES: *Steep hills, dramatic*
SOLITUDE: ✿ ✿ ✿	*views, parkland meadows, and abundant blueberries*

This is one of the more spectacular hikes in the Snoqualmie Pass area. Proximity to Seattle makes it an ideal destination if you want to slip away for a day or just a long afternoon. This trail has lots to engage children's interest and plenty of convenient turnaround spots if they get tired. Be aware that the last 0.25 miles (from the ridge crest) is somewhat exposed.

🚶 This hike starts out heading north along the PCT. The trail gradually climbs through an old-growth forest of fir and hemlock, a good distraction from the I-90 corridor traffic. The sound of speeding cars is soon replaced by the gurgle of creeks and the chirping of songbirds as the trail wraps around a ridge and enters Alpine Lakes Wilderness.

After 2.5 miles the trail reaches a junction. The PCT continues climbing toward Kendall Ridge, while Commonwealth Basin Trail branches to the left and gradually descends into an open meadow. Meandering streams, small stands of trees, pockets of wildflowers, and creekside campsites are just a few of the treasures to look forward to.

After 4 miles you cross Commonwealth Creek, which is usually dry by mid- to late summer. Earlier in the season you can easily wade through the shallow water or cautiously rock-hop across.

Once you have crossed the creek, the real climb begins. Tight, short switchbacks follow a narrow ridge for 500 feet, making this a steep ascent. However, you're rewarded with an amazing view about halfway up the ridge, with Guye Peak, Cave Ridge, and Alpental Ski

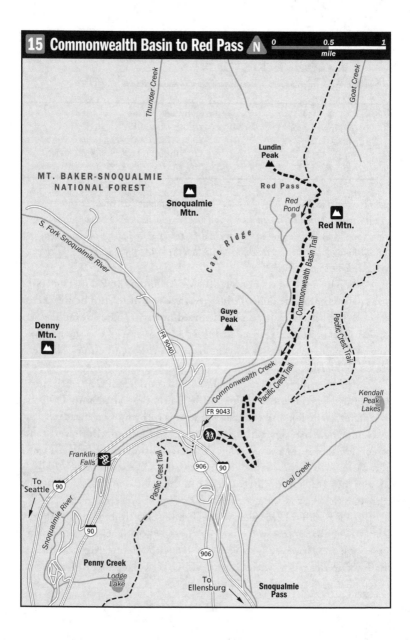

0   0.5   1
mile

Thunder Creek

Goat Creek

MT. BAKER-SNOQUALMIE
NATIONAL FOREST

Lundin
Peak

Red Pass

Snoqualmie
Mtn.

Red
Pond

Red Mtn.

C a v e   R i d g e

S. Fork Snoqualmie River

Commonwealth Basin Trail

Pacific Crest Trail

Guye
Peak

Denny
Mtn.

FR 9040

Commonwealth Creek

Pacific Crest Trail

Kendall
Peak
Lakes

FR 9043

Franklin
Falls

Pacific Crest Trail

906

90

Coal Creek

To
Seattle

90

Snoqualmie River

906

Penny Creek

Lodge
Lake

To
Ellensburg

Snoqualmie
Pass

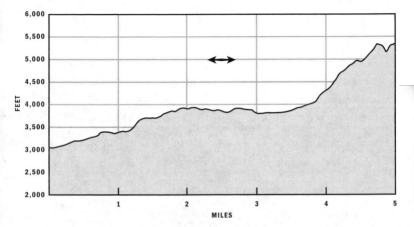

Area to the southwest, and the broad slopes of Snoqualmie Mountain to the northwest. This spot is also the perfect place to catch your breath and take in some of the seasonal riches of this area, such as June's trilliums, whose colors range from white to violet; July's bright-red scarlet paintbrush; and August's bumper crop of blueberries.

The trail's grade gradually eases as it approaches Red Pond, a good spot to rest on a boulder on a lazy afternoon. From here you also have a great view of the deep-red, rocky slopes of Red Mountain. For those continuing on to the pass, take the second spur trail that you passed as you approached the pond on your way up. The trail makes a couple of long switchbacks before traveling through open talus slopes on its course approximately 200 feet above the pond. If you are doing this hike early in the season, be aware that snow lingers on this west-facing slope, which can make the trail difficult to follow and easy to slip on.

After a long ascent, the trail enters a stand of subalpine firs and switchbacks to the crest of the ridge, where you get stunning views of

Mt. Thompson dominates the foreground from Red Pass.

the valley and a sea of peaks beyond. Follow the trail as it descends slightly to a short series of switchbacks to Red Pass (5,350 feet).

If you are looking for a good lunch spot with a breathtaking view, there are a few side trails branching north off the main trail, just before you reach the pass. Try to take the most-used path, which ascends 100 feet to a high point. From there, the views to the north are dramatic, to say the least, with steep, rocky slopes and cascading creeks tumbling toward the deep gorges of the Middle Fork of the Snoqualmie River. Mount Thompson dominates the view to the northeast, its massive form jutting out from a series of craggy ridgelines and imposing peaks. The Snoqualmie Ski Area, resembling a tiny village that might be found somewhere in the Alps, is visible to the south.

If you're feeling adventurous, an unmaintained trail leads to the summit of Lundin Peak (6,057 feet). The "trail," which is really more of a climber's path, heads east from Red Pass and ascends steeply through benches of heather and small rock outcroppings. The summit is 0.5 miles up, and if your heart isn't already pumping, it will be when you peek over the edge at the vertical drop-off the northwest side of the peak. The views from this craggy perch are well worth the extra effort, with Snoqualmie Mountain's broad slopes to the west and Lake Keechelus's long, narrow shorelines to the south. Although this trail is relatively well traveled, it is really more of a scramble than a hike; early in the season bring an ice axe.

DIRECTIONS   Follow I-90 to Snoqualmie Pass and take Exit 52 if you are coming from the west and Exit 53 if coming from the east. Turn north onto Alpental Road, go under the freeway, and immediately turn on to the spur road branching to the right. Follow the signs to the PCT parking area.

PERMIT   Northwest Forest Pass required. Self-issued permits available at trailhead.

GPS Trailhead Coordinates	15 Commonwealth Basin to Red Pass
UTM Zone (WGS 84)	10T
Easting	0619651
Northing	5253926
Latitude	N47.427802°
Longitude	W121.413448°

16 Spectacle Lake

SCENERY: ✿ ✿ ✿ ✿

TRAIL CONDITION: ✿ ✿ ✿

CHILDREN: ✿ ✿ ✿ ✿ ✿ (to Pete Lake)

DIFFICULTY: ✿ ✿ ✿

SOLITUDE: ✿ ✿ ✿

DISTANCE: 20 miles

HIKING TIME: 2–3 days

GREEN TRAILS MAPS: Kachess Lake 208 and Snoqualmie Pass 207

OUTSTANDING FEATURES: An old-growth forest; a great first lake to take kids on an overnight; and, for those willing to put in a little extra effort, a glacier-carved lake encircled by jagged peaks

This hike is broken into two very different legs. The first leg takes you to a peaceful little lake called Pete. Mostly flat and heavily used by horsepackers and hikers alike, this is great for beginning backpackers or families with kids. The second leg gains 1,300 feet (most of that in the last few miles) on its way to the secluded, glacier-polished shores of Spectacle Lake. This hiker-only lake offers excellent mountain views and is more than worth the additional exertion.

🏃🏃 This hike begins in a tranquil setting at the far northwest corner of Cooper Lake. From the trailhead, Pete Lake Trail 1323 gently rolls through stands of old-growth Douglas fir and hemlock, paralleling Cooper River, which for much of the hike cannot be seen or heard. The trail gains a mere 300 feet on its 4.5-mile journey to Pete Lake, making it a great destination for those with kids.

As you leave the trailhead (elevation 2,800 feet), take note of the crystal-clear pools of the Cooper River. The trail quickly strays from the slow-moving water and enters the cool shade of the forest canopy. At 1.4 miles the trail meets up with Tired Creek Trail 1317, which branches to the northeast en route to Waptus Lake. Remain on Pete Lake Trail and in another 0.5 miles enter Alpine Lakes Wilderness.

At 3.1 miles there is a campsite just off the trail, if you are looking to escape the crowds for a night. Beyond the site, the trail turns away from the river, passes a meadow, and, in another mile, crosses a couple of rocky side streams that are usually dry by late summer

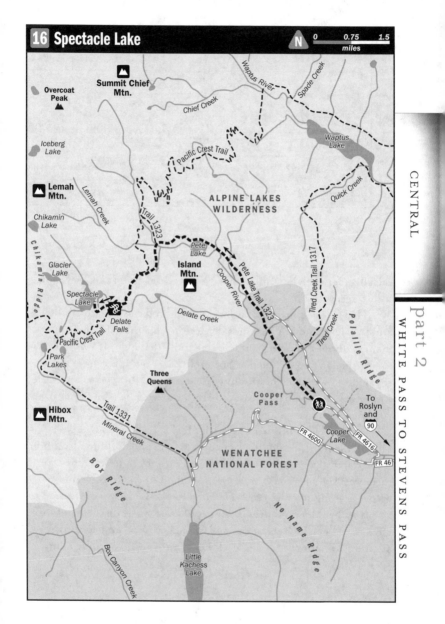

Overcoat
Peak

Summit Chief
Mtn.

Chief Creek

Waptus River

Spade Creek

Iceberg
Lake

Pacific Crest Trail

Waptus
Lake

Lemah
Mtn.

Chikamin
Lake

Lemah Creek

Trail 1323

ALPINE LAKES
WILDERNESS

Quick Creek

Glacier
Lake

Pete
Lake

Spectacle
Lake

Island
Mtn.

Cooper River

Pete Lake Trail 1323

Tired Creek Trail 1317

Delate
Falls

Delate Creek

Tired Creek

Pacific Crest Trail

Park
Lakes

Polallie Ridge

Three
Queens

Cooper
Pass

To
Roslyn and

90

Hibox
Mtn.

Trail 1331

Mineral Creek

Cooper Pass

FR 4600

Cooper
Lake

FR 4616

FR 46

WENATCHEE
NATIONAL FOREST

No Name Ridge

Box Ridge

Box Canyon Creek

Little
Kachess
Lake

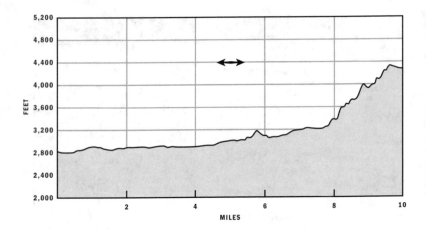

or fall. A leisurely 4.5 miles later, you arrive at Pete Lake, elevation 2,980 feet.

This forested little lake is hard to beat in terms of accessibility, and the views into the Lemah Range create an alpinelike environment, without requiring you to climb quite that high. It's not nearly as breathtaking or secluded as Spectacle Lake, but it is a great option if you don't want to schlep your pack another 1,300 feet to Spectacle. Either way, it's the perfect spot to enjoy lunch while contemplating your next move.

If you decide to continue (which I highly recommend), hike around the north side of the lake, bypassing the turnoff for Escondido Lake/Waptus Pass. As you leave the lake's shrubby shoreline, the trail turns west and begins a 2-mile ascent of the Lemah Creek drainage before arriving at a nice creekside camp tucked in a stand of trees.

If water is low and the crossing looks safe, wade or rock-hop your way across Lemah Creek at the well-signed crossing and continue another 0.8 miles to the PCT. If the water is high, continue along

Lemah Meadow Trail 1323B to the PCT and cross the creek on a footbridge, adding 1 mile in each direction to your hike.

The PCT remains forested and fairly flat for the next 0.5 miles. Glancing eastward you catch glimpses of Delate Meadows, motivating you on your climb into the high country. Long, somewhat relentless switchbacks wind back and forth, offering occasional views of Chikamin Ridge and Three Queens Mountain (elevation 6,687 feet).

Just before you reach the 9-mile mark, the trail reaches Delate Falls, a spectacular place to take a well-earned break. From here you have two alternatives for getting to Spectacle Lake. The first is to ascend a hard-to-find and overgrown shortcut known as "The Staircase." The trail heads right just after the last switchback before the Delate Falls footbridge and is really more of a root-and-rock scramble. But it cuts 0.5 miles from the hike, and rewards you with another waterfall that pours from the outlet at the eastern end of the lake.

If you're carrying a big pack or the trail is slick, feel free to take the much mellower PCT another mile past the footbridge to the second turnoff for Spectacle Lake. This option adds about 100 feet of elevation gain but is more likely to get you there without any hitches. Descend to the lake along a hiker-only trail that is fairly steep and rutted, passing granite outcroppings scattered through fields of huckleberry bushes and squatty evergreens.

Arriving at Spectacle Lake (elevation 4,239 feet), you will most likely forget the pain in your legs and the kink in your neck as you gaze out at the crystal-clear waters that seem to extend in every direction toward the mighty peaks that surround it. A maze of social trails guides you across glacier-polished rock to a finger of land that juts out on the south side of the lake. There are excellent campsites throughout this area, and like all alpine treasures, the vegetation is fragile, so please do your part to preserve it.

Views from this camp are anything but disappointing. The longest arm of the lake stretches north toward the spires, mini-arêtes,

The tranquil waters of Pete Lake

and hanging glaciers that comprise Lemah Peak, the most dramatically aesthetic peak in the cirque. Southwest of Lemah is Chikamin Peak, and south of that extends rugged Chikamin Ridge. Glacier and Chikamin lakes lie west and north of Spectacle, further evidence of the retreating glaciers that carved out this beautiful landscape.

If you have the time, spend more than one night in this area. One great approach is to spend your first night down low, either at Pete Lake or along Lemah Creek, then get an early start on your second day and set up camp at Spectacle Lake. If time and energy permit, a strong hiker can get back on the southbound PCT and day hike 4.5 miles farther, to Chikamin Pass (elevation 5,780 feet), where alpine vistas await. Even without hiking to Chikamin Pass, you will want to spend as much time as possible soaking up the gorgeous high country that surrounds Spectacle Lake.

DIRECTIONS   From I-90 eastbound take Exit 80 toward Roslyn, Salmon La Sac. Turn left at the top of the off-ramp. Follow the road 2.7 miles and turn left at a T-junction onto WA 903 north. Drive through Roslyn, following the signs for Salmon La Sac.

Follow this road 14.5 miles from Roslyn and turn left onto FR 46, following the signs for Cooper Lake. Cross the Cle Elum River and, in 4.7 miles, turn right onto FR 4616, signed PETE LAKE TRAIL. Cross the outlet bridge, turn left, and drive another 2 miles to the trailhead at the northwest corner of Cooper Lake.

PERMIT   Northwest Forest Pass required. Self-issued permits available at trailhead.

GPS Trailhead Coordinates	16 Spectacle Lake
UTM Zone (WGS 84)	10T
Easting	0636708
Northing	5255008
Latitude	N47.434181°
Longitude	W121.187058°

SCENERY: ✿ ✿ ✿ ✿	DISTANCE: *14.5 miles*
TRAIL CONDITION: ✿ ✿ ✿	HIKING TIME: *7 hours or 2 days*
CHILDREN: ✿ ✿ ✿	GREEN TRAILS MAP: Stevens Pass 176
✿ ✿ ✿ ✿ ✿ *(to Hyas Lake)*	OUTSTANDING FEATURES: *Steep creeks,*
DIFFICULTY: ✿ ✿ ✿ ✿	*rugged terrain, sparkling alpine lakes, and big,*
SOLITUDE: ✿ ✿ ✿	*beautiful mountains*

This loop hike can be done in one somewhat strenuous day—but this is one of my favorite sections in Alpine Lakes Wilderness and rushing through it would be regrettable. There are multiple backpacking options, including a couple of lakes that are great for novices or families wanting to bring along the kids.

🚶 The first 0.25 miles of the trail follows an abandoned road. A sturdy bridge provides access over the Cle Elum River and marks the start of the true trail to Cathedral Pass. From here the trail quickly enters the cool shade of the forest canopy, which can provide much-needed relief as you begin a moderate but steady climb toward Squaw Lake. In 0.5 miles the trail crosses into Alpine Lakes Wilderness, where fires are prohibited above 5,000 feet and at the popular but fragile shores of Deep Lake (elevation 4,380 feet).

Beyond the boundary, the trail resumes its ascent up lengthy switchbacks through a forest of sweet-smelling pines. In 2.1 miles you reach the turnoff for Waptus and Michael lakes along Trail Creek Trail 1322. Continue on Trail 1345 toward Squaw Lake and Cathedral Pass. Just beyond the junction, you leave the switchbacks behind as the trail begins a steep 0.25-mile climb straight up the hillside. At 2.4 miles the trail flattens back out, allowing you to catch your breath and enjoy the next 0.25 miles to the lake.

The trail pops out in marshy meadows at Squaw Lake's northeast shoreline. With good picnicking spots and smaller crowds than at Hyas

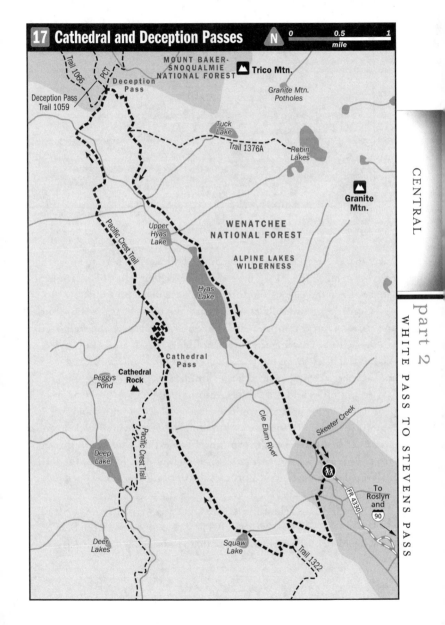

Trail 1086

PCT

MOUNT BAKER-
SNOQUALMIE
NATIONAL FOREST

Trico Mtn.

Deception
Pass

Granite Mtn.
Potholes

Deception Pass
Trail 1059

Tuck
Lake

Trail 1376A

Robin
Lakes

Pacific Crest Trail

Upper
Hyas
Lake

Granite
Mtn.

WENATCHEE
NATIONAL FOREST

ALPINE LAKES
WILDERNESS

Hyas
Lake

Cathedral Pass

Peggys
Pond

Cathedral
Rock

Pacific Crest Trail

Deep
Lake

Cle Elum River

Skeeter Creek

To
Roslyn
and
90

FR 4330

Deer
Lakes

Squaw
Lake

Trail 1322

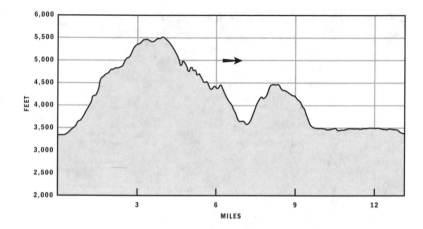

Lake, this is a great option for a mellow day hike: It's hard to go wrong relaxing at an alpine lake. There are also excellent tent-site locations, set back from the lake's shoreline, and a designated pit toilet.

Continuing toward Cathedral Pass, the trail skirts the shoreline and passes a horse camp, at the lake's inlet. From here the trail begins another climb, crossing the inlet a couple of times along the way. As the trail rises above the lake, the terrain takes on a more rugged appearance, weaving around large boulders.

At 3.2 miles and 5,000 feet, another sign warns that fires are prohibited in the area. As you continue, you are enter a subalpine region; the trees are shorter and the huckleberry bushes thicker, and clumps of heather cover the ground. The next mile takes you through gorgeous meadows and past small snowmelt ponds. Much of the trail is elevated on boardwalks to protect the delicate and sometimes soggy vegetation below.

Cathedral Pass (elevation 5,620 feet) is 4.5 miles from the trailhead; here you meet up with the PCT. The pass sits near the base of Cathedral Rock, a formidable peak that rises sharply from the parkland meadows surrounding it. The view from here is powerful, to say the least, so an out-and-back hike would be far from disappointing. There is also ample cross-country exploring to do from here, with lots of great camping. Making a day hike—heading 3 miles from a camp at the pass to Deep Lake—would round out a wonderful three-day weekend.

To continue the loop to Deception Pass, turn north when you arrive at the PCT. If you decide on this option, be warned that there are two creeks pouring from the icy slopes of Mount Daniel, and these can be treacherous to cross during times of peak snowmelt or heavy rain. Many backpackers have been forced to turn around at these rivers; check with the Forest Service if you are concerned about conditions.

As you descend from Cathedral Pass, the trail remains in the shadow of Cathedral Peak, its silhouette transforming as you wrap around its eastern flank. A narrow valley filled with car-sized boulders separates you from this daunting rock formation. The trail loses elevation quickly down tight switchbacks that wind through stands of hemlocks and swaths of huckleberries. Before you know it, you are back in the forest, making long, gentle switchbacks once again.

At 5.8 miles, the trail comes to a small clearing that provides a bird's-eye view of Hyas and Upper Hyas lakes. The views come and go as you continue descending toward a large boulder field. At the toe of the boulders, two creeks converge; you'll find shady, creekside campsites here. Water can be somewhat sparse at the crossing in late summer or early fall, but just downstream from the sites is a year-round source.

The trail continues its descent down valley through a hodgepodge of mountain hemlock, Douglas fir, alder, and red cedar. Less than 1 mile from the first creek, you reach another. Beyond the crossing, the trail crosses numerous avalanche slide paths that can be overgrown and brushy. The magnitude of these slides is evidenced by the hundreds of trees littering the valley floor like matchsticks.

The trail soon reaches the first of two sketchy creek crossings. The power of the creek can be felt, even in low water, as it comes roaring through a rocky slot canyon just above the point where you cross it. You may be able to find a semi-safe crossing along fallen trees; however, plan to get your shoes wet and be happy if you don't have to.

After safely crossing the creek, begin the climb to Deception Pass. In 1 mile the trail turns east and hits the second major creek, at the head of the Cle Elum River valley. The crossing can be nothing more than a simple rock hop late in the season; regardless, use caution because the rocks are slippery and taking a spill this far from the trailhead would definitely ruin your day.

Beyond the creek the trail keeps climbing, passing a small pond with a couple of campsites lacking views before reaching the broad, forested saddle known as Deception Pass (elevation 4,475 feet). From the pass, you have a couple of routes to choose among. The PCT continues its journey north-northeast, Marmot Lake Trail 1066 branches 3.5 miles to the west, and Deception Creek Trail 1059 goes north to Highway 2, ending about 6 miles outside the town of Skykomish.

To finish the loop, head down the Cle Elum River drainage along Trail 1376. As you descend, crazy assortments of colorful fungi pop up trailside. Avid mushroom hunters come from near and far to harvest these delectable treats during the peak picking season. Even if mushrooms aren't your area of expertise, their interesting shapes and slimy texture will fascinate you.

In a little more than 0.5 miles, the trail intersects the turnoff for Tuck and Robin lakes. These alpine gems have been compared in beauty to those that lie in the heavily regulated Enchantment region. Because no permits are required, these lakes are in jeopardy of being

Fall foliage along a small tarn near Cathedral Pass

loved to death. If you decide to explore this area (which I advise doing on a weekday), use preexisting campsites and social trails and bring a stove: Campfires are prohibited.

Continuing on Trail 1376, a mile-long, knee-pounding descent brings you to the valley floor. You cross several small streams and rocky creeks en route to the swampy shoreline of Upper Hyas Lake. From here you can see your entire route from Cathedral Rock to the head of the Cle Elum River, with immense Mount Daniel dominating the background. The camping around the lake is less than ideal, with a couple horsy-smelling sites and muddy access to the water.

Just beyond the upper lake's outlet lies Hyas Lake. An easy 1.5 miles from the trailhead parking lot, this mile-long lake has abundant campsites (and pit toilets) for people looking to "get their feet

wet" in the backpacking world. As you pass the sites, you can hear
young kids splashing in the nearby water and novice backpackers saying things like, "I thought you brought the poles." The lake has the
same stunning views as Upper Hyas, so it's no wonder these sites are
packed. If you're looking for solitude, camp at any of the lakes mentioned earlier in the description.

Leaving the lake, the trail becomes a wide, heavily used path,
a sign that the majority of the people in this area come to stay at
Hyas Lakes. The ground is fairly level, making the last stretch of this
14-mile hike pleasant. Make sure to leave some time on the drive
home to check out the town of Roslyn, made famous by the 1990s hit
TV show *Northern Exposure.*

DIRECTIONS From I-90 eastbound, take Exit 80 toward Roslyn,
Salmon La Sac. Turn left at the top of the off ramp. Follow the road 2.7
miles and turn left at a T-junction onto WA 903 north. Drive through
Roslyn, following signs for Salmon La Sac. In 16.7 miles the road forks.
Veer right, onto FR 4330 toward Tucquala Lake. In 7.6 miles you'll
reach the Scatter Creek ford, which could present a problem in high
water if you have a low-clearance vehicle. Continue past the ford another
5 miles to the road's end. Both trailheads are located in the large parking area.

PERMIT Northwest Forest Pass required. Self-issued permits available at trailhead.

GPS Trailhead Coordinates	17 Cathedral and Deception Passes
UTM Zone (WGS 84)	10T
Easting	0643217
Northing	5267292
Latitude	N47.543250°
Longitude	W121.096798°

18 Surprise and Glacier Lakes

SCENERY: ✿ ✿ ✿ ✿
TRAIL CONDITION: ✿ ✿ ✿ ✿
CHILDREN: ✿ ✿
DIFFICULTY: ✿ ✿ ✿
SOLITUDE: ✿ ✿
DISTANCE: *10 miles*

HIKING TIME: *6–7 hours or overnight*
GREEN TRAILS MAP: Stevens Pass 176
OUTSTANDING FEATURES: *A creekside hike through a mossy forest, two alpine lakes, and spectacular views of surrounding peaks*

This classic westside hike is accessible rain or shine. Even on a cold, drippy day, when the mountaintops are shrouded in mist, the forest takes on a mystical feel, with its moss-covered rocks, mushroom-speckled trees, and crystal-clear creek. Once you have ascended from the valley, you are rewarded with two splendid alpine lakes with great shoreline campsites. If you head out on a weekend, be prepared to share these gems with others—their proximity to Seattle makes them a hot destination.

🚶🚶 As you begin this hike, you may wonder, "Where are all of those wonderful old-growth trees?" Don't worry—you'll see them soon enough. First you have to get up a steep, heart-pumping, rutted-out road; pass under enormous, buzzing power lines; and, in 0.25 miles, arrive at the official trailhead for Surprise Lake Trail 1060 (elevation 2,200 feet).

The trail branches south off the road, immediately entering a thick forest full of monster hemlock, Douglas fir, and cedar. A boardwalk keeps you above the waterlogged muck that makes up the forest floor, a sign of the massive amount of precipitation this area receives. You'll hear occasional whistle blasts from the train rolling through the valley, giving the hike an old-time feel.

In 0.5 miles the trail reaches a snag dotted with slimy mushrooms, which marks the entrance into Alpine Lakes Wilderness. From here the trail continues its gradual ascent, offering occasional glimpses into the crystal-clear, icy-cold waters of Surprise Creek. Cross it on a log at 1.2 miles to find excellent creekside campsites.

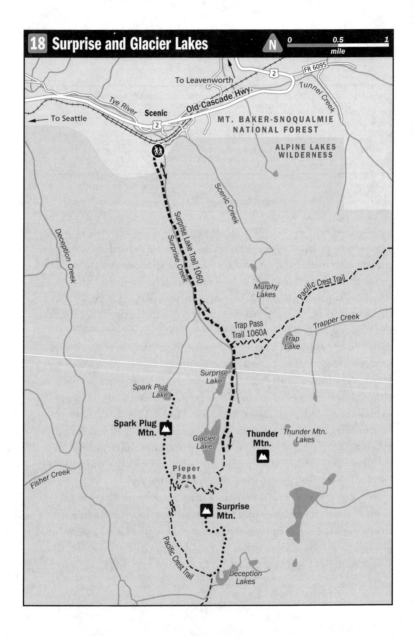

18 Surprise and Glacier Lakes

N 0 0.5 1
mile

To Leavenworth

2 FR 6095

Tye River Scenic Old Cascade Hwy.

Tunnel Creek

← To Seattle 2

MT. BAKER-SNOQUALMIE
NATIONAL FOREST

ALPINE LAKES
WILDERNESS

Scenic Creek

Deception Creek

Surprise Lake Trail 1060

Surprise Creek

Murphy Lakes

Pacific Crest Trail

Trapper Creek

Trap Pass
Trail 1060A

Trap Lake

Surprise Lake

Spark Plug Lake

Spark Plug Mtn.

Glacier Lake

Thunder Mtn.

Thunder Mtn. Lakes

Fisher Creek

Pieper Pass

Surprise Mtn.

Pacific Crest Trail

Deception Lakes

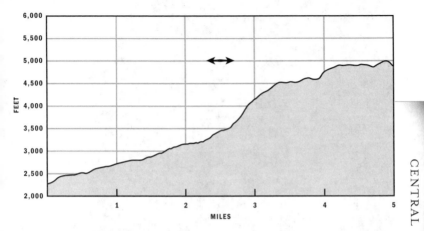

This next section takes you through a broad valley, where snow slides roar from steep slopes to the east and west of the drainage. Follow the trail past a large boulder with a mossy micro-forest sprouting from it. A bit farther you cross the toe of an avalanche path, where large rocks sit among an entanglement of devil's club and slide alder.

At 1.6 miles the trail arrives at another creekside camp. One site has room for two small tents. The trail sticks close to the creek for another 0.75 miles and then switchbacks up the east side of the valley. As you climb, vistas begin to open to the west, toward an unnamed cirque north of Spark Plug Mountain. You continue to climb for the next 2 miles before arriving at the creek once again. The trail parallels the boulder-choked waters for 0.5 miles before reaching a junction with Trap Pass Trail 1060A. This trail eventually grinds its way up to the PCT, gaining 700 feet in 0.6 miles.

For those looking for a slightly easier path to the PCT, follow the signs to Surprise Lake. The trail crosses Surprise Creek on a confusing maze of social trails and soon arrives at the lake's northeast shore (elevation 4,508 feet). This is one of the more heavily used lakes in the area, so please camp at designated sites and observe any closures

Mushrooms take root on a moss-covered stump.

or restoration efforts in the area. If you are out for the day, there is a wonderful picnic rock just off the trail that wraps around the east side of the lake.

From Surprise Lake, continue south as the trail rises away from the lakeshore. Follow a rib, and, in 0.5 miles, you arrive at the PCT.

Continue south past a narrow pond and in less than 0.25 miles the trail begins a traverse 50 to 100 feet above the rockbound shores of Glacier Lake (elevation 4,806 feet). There is no official sign for the lake, so keep an eye out for a trail that branches to the west.

The deep-blue water of Glacier Lake, which lies in the shadow of Spark Plug Mountain (elevation 6,311 feet), is gorgeous, with great camping among sparse trees on the east bank. Once you have settled in, there are a few options for further exploration.

Continue south on the PCT from Glacier Lake to the 6,000-foot Pieper Pass. From here you can head north cross-country to Spark Plug Mountain and Spark Plug Lake, or continue along the PCT another 2 miles to Deception Lake. Extremely motivated, strong hikers can climb another 1.3 miles from the lakes to the top of Surprise Mountain (elevation 6,330 feet), where stunning views of the glaciated slopes of Mount Daniel await. When you have had your fill of this stunning country, retrace your route to the trailhead.

DIRECTIONS From Seattle, head east on US 2 toward Stevens Pass. Continue 0.7 miles past milepost 58 to an unmarked road. Turn south toward the service center for Burlington Northern Railroad. Cross the railroad tracks and turn right. Continue another 0.1 mile, following a hiker sign to the trailhead. A steep, narrow road continues beyond the main parking area, but it is not worth getting your car stuck in an effort to avoid a mere 0.2 miles of walking.

PERMIT Northwest Forest Pass required. Self-issued permits available at trailhead.

GPS Trailhead Coordinates	18 Surprise and Glacier Lakes
UTM Zone (WGS 84)	10T
Easting	0638270
Northing	5285174
Latitude	N47.705143°
Longitude	W121.156855°

19 Hope and Mig Lakes

SCENERY: ✰ ✰ ✰	HIKING TIME: *3 hours*
TRAIL CONDITION: ✰ ✰ ✰	GREEN TRAILS MAP: Stevens Pass 176
CHILDREN: ✰ ✰ ✰	OUTSTANDING FEATURES: *Quick, easy access*
DIFFICULTY: ✰ ✰ ✰	*to Alpine Lakes Wilderness, good huckleberry picking,*
SOLITUDE: ✰ ✰ ✰	*and an opportunity to explore a variety of lakes scat-*
DISTANCE: *4 miles*	*tered north and south along the PCT*

This trail's proximity to Seattle and relatively quick access into Alpine Lakes Wilder-
ness made me wonder, "Where are all the people?" As I hit the trail, my thighs imme-
diately began to burn. I soon came to realize that the trailhead, located just before
the road begins its climb to Stevens Pass, intimidates many hikers. Although you can
access some lakes with a bit less elevation gain, if you're willing to sweat a bit more,
this short, sweet hike will reward you in the end.

👫 This trail gets your heart pumping from the beginning with
a steep, dusty climb through an old clear-cut before entering the
cool shade of the forest. Douglas fir, hemlock, and a few old cedars
keep you company as you steadily make your way up the valley. In
0.25 miles the trail crosses a small footbridge in a large patch of
huckleberry bushes. If you are here in late July or August, make sure
to leave time to collect a midmorning snack or an afternoon treat.

Once you have had your fair share of berry goodness, continue
your ascent through the woods. At 0.5 miles a 15- to 20-foot cliff-
band intersects the trail. A short, but precarious path branches off
from here, providing a view into a mini-gorge through which Tunnel Creek bubbles; however, the view from the main trail is just as
impressive.

From here, the trail wraps around the backside of the rock formation, keeping Tunnel Creek out of sight for another 0.5 miles. In
0.25 miles the trail cuts through a swath of alders interspersed with
devil's club, a tall, thorny plant that can bring the most hardcore of

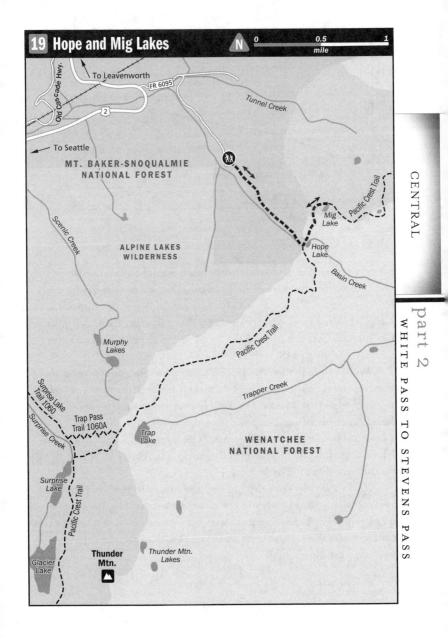

N

0   0.5   1
mile

To Leavenworth

FR 6095

Old Cascade Hwy.

2

Tunnel Creek

To Seattle

MT. BAKER-SNOQUALMIE
NATIONAL FOREST

Pacific Crest Trail

CENTRAL

Mig Lake

Scenic Creek

ALPINE LAKES
WILDERNESS

Hope Lake

Basin Creek

Murphy Lakes

Pacific Crest Trail

Trapper Creek

Surprise Lake Trail 1060

Trap Pass Trail 1060A

Trap Lake

WENATCHEE
NATIONAL FOREST

Surprise Creek

Surprise Lake

Pacific Crest Trail

Glacier Lake

Thunder Mtn.

Thunder Mtn. Lakes

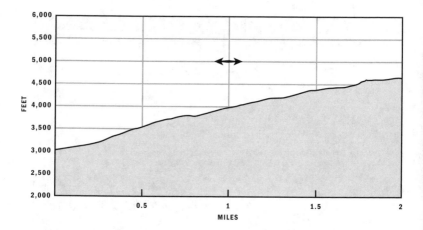

hikers to tears if they stumble into them. Soon you reenter the forest and cross a couple of small, steep creeks that are usually dry by mid- to late summer. Even without water, these drainages are impressive. Large, downed trees are strewn throughout the creekbed, crisscrossed like matchsticks, evidence of the large, wet avalanches that can rip through the area in the winter and early spring months.

An old slide path at the 1-mile mark provides another glimpse of Tunnel Creek. From here it is a short climb back through the forest to Alpine Lakes Wilderness boundary and the opaque waters of Hope Lake. A couple of smaller ponds are visible through the trees from a bench above the lake to the south. The large campsites around the lake will most likely be taken on the weekends. There's a vault toilet on the west side of the lake.

If you want to take a dip but feel the murky waters of Hope Lake are uninviting, head north to the clearer waters of Mig Lake. It's a quick trip, with a climb of just more than 300 feet in 0.5 miles. The trail wanders through a forest of fir and hemlock before topping out in a large meadow.

The forested shoreline of Mig Lake

The trail slowly contours to the east through the parkland as it makes its way around the north side of the lake. As you approach the shoreline, keep an eye out for a well-used spur trail that branches right. The trail passes a lily-pad-filled pond before arriving at an overlook that also works well for picnics. The PCT continues around the north side of the lake, crossing a quaint stream that snakes through grasslands and marshy fields. There are a couple good campsites on the northeast side of the lake (same side as the vault toilet). If you plan to camp at Hope or Mig lakes, be aware that campfires are prohibited within 0.5 miles of the lakes.

If you want to spend an entire day in this area, you have a couple options, depending on how much time and energy you have. Two miles north of Mig Lake is Swimming Deer Lake, and north of that lies the large, forested shores of Josephine Lake. If you can arrange transportation, you can continue north on the PCT, past Lake Susan Jane to Stevens Pass (7.5 miles from Mig Lake).

Heading south on the PCT from Hope Lake, the trail travels almost 4 miles along a ridge with great views to sparkling Trap Lake. If you are fortunate enough to have an extra vehicle, you can arrange another thru-hike: From Trap Lake, descend southwest to trail 1060A and switchback steeply to the long, narrow Surprise Lake. Continue north on Trail 1060, a hiker-only route through the lush drainage of Surprise Creek (Hike 18, page 125).

DIRECTIONS   Head east on US 2 toward Stevens Pass. Continue 12 miles past the quiet town of Skykomish, cross the Tunnel Creek Bridge, and, just beyond the hairpin, turn right onto FR 6095. At 0.8 miles you will reach a junction; go straight. At 1.2 miles the road splits, take the left branch and head up the steep road. The trailhead for Tunnel Creek Trail 1061 is 0.1 mile along, on the right side of the road.

NOTE: This trailhead is accessible only from the eastbound lane. If you are driving west on US 2, continue past the trailhead, find a safe spot to turn around, and head back east to FR 6095.

PERMIT   Northwest Forest Pass required. Self-issued permits available at trailhead.

GPS Trailhead Coordinates	19 Hope and Mig Lakes
UTM Zone (WGS 84)	10T
Easting	0641672
Northing	5285962
Latitude	N47.711486°
Longitude	W121.111272°

20 Chain and Doelle Lakes

SCENERY: ✿ ✿ ✿ ✿	HIKING TIME: *3–4 days*
TRAIL CONDITION: ✿ ✿ ✿	GREEN TRAILS MAPS: Stevens Pass 176 *and* Chiwaukum Mountains 177
CHILDREN: ✿	OUTSTANDING FEATURES: *Parkland meadows, views into some of the most remote areas in the Central Cascades, a multitude of alpine lakes—and solitude at the most stunning of these*
DIFFICULTY: ✿ ✿ ✿ ✿	
SOLITUDE: ✿ ✿ ✿	
DISTANCE: 22 miles	

A good friend and former Forest Service employee described this trip as including "one of the best alpine lakes in the Central Cascades." And even though I scouted them in a torrential downpour, I agree with him: The lakes are amazing, and the solitude is worth every switchback. To get the most out of your trip, give yourself time to explore the high country surrounding this truly magical place.

🚶🚶 Your first 4 miles of hiking are going to be a far cry from a wilderness experience; busy trails, buzzing power lines, screaming chainsaws, and multiple ski lifts are just a few of the distractions you are likely to encounter. You are traveling through a ski area, after all.

That said, plenty of nature's distractions—such as fat, juicy huckleberries, the high-pitched whistle of a marmot as it waddles away to hide, and morning dewdrops in the leaf of a lupine—make this stretch enjoyable. Besides, the remaining 7 miles to the lakes more than make up for the fact that the first few are less than ideal. Take this section for what it is and know that the best is yet to come.

The PCT begins with a short but steep hike into a nice stand of timber. You gradually reach open slopes and catch sight of the first-cut ski run at Stevens Pass. The original ski area, which differed drastically from what you see today, was developed back in 1937 by two avid skiers named Don Adams and Bruce Kehr. The two men obtained

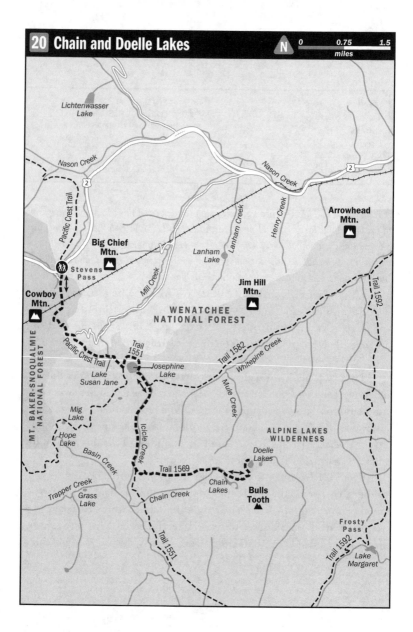

N

0   0.75   1.5
miles

Lichtenwasser
Lake

Nason Creek

Nason Creek

Pacific Crest Trail

Arrowhead
Mtn.

Big Chief
Mtn.

Lanham Creek

Henry Creek

Lanham
Lake

Stevens
Pass

Mill Creek

Jim Hill
Mtn.

Cowboy
Mtn.

WENATCHEE
NATIONAL FOREST

Pacific Crest Trail

Trail
1551

Trail 1582

Whitepine Creek

Trail 1592

Lake
Susan Jane

Josephine
Lake

MT. BAKER-SNOQUALMIE
NATIONAL FOREST

Mig
Lake

Mule Creek

ALPINE LAKES
WILDERNESS

Hope
Lake

Basin Creek

Icicle Creek

Doelle
Lakes

Trail 1569

Chain
Lakes

Bulls
Tooth

Trapper Creek

Grass
Lake

Chain Creek

Frosty
Pass

Trail 1551

Trail 1592

Lake
Margaret

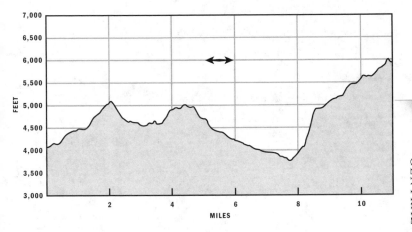

a permit from the Forest Service, cut a small swath, bought supplies to build a $600 rope tow, and opened for business, charging skiers 5 cents for each ride up the tow.

At the time you had two choices: make a 6-mile hike on the highway from the small town of Scenic, or purchase a one-way ticket on the Great Northern Passenger train, then hop an old school bus to the ski area. Eventually four rope tows were installed, but they were replaced in 1964 by the two-person chair you see today. The trail crosses under the chair, leaving the meadow and a bit of Stevens Pass history behind.

The trees for the next mile or so create a sight and sound barrier from the highway below and also provide shade, a welcome relief on a hot, buggy day. In 1.5 miles you cross under the Tye Mill chair and begin a steady series of switchbacks. The trail ascends in the shadow of Cowboy Ridge, a recreational hotspot for backcountry skiers and snowboarders looking to test their skills in its steep, rocky terrain.

After a somewhat grinding climb you eventually reach the ridgetop (elevation 5,120 feet), just east of the backside chairlift that

Lakeside camping at Chain Lakes

descends into Mill Valley. Immediate views from this location aren't that impressive; however, once you get beyond the power lines and chairlifts, the views of what lies ahead should excite you. From here you can also see your route etched in a hillside far below.

To get there, descend a couple of rocky switchbacks and continue southeastward, as the trail travels below a long ridgeline known as Rooster Comb. As you make your way to the wilderness boundary, you encounter a few more artificial obstacles. At 3.3 miles, the trail cuts under the chairlift, goes through a boulder field, and pops out on a service road. Follow the signs across the road and resume your hike, heading under large, crackling power lines.

A short way from here is the Alpine Lakes Wilderness boundary. From this point it is less than 1 mile to your first alpine lake, Susan

Jane. The trail arrives at the south shore, which has good camping—a decent option if you have kids or time constraints. The area can be busy on weekends, so be prepared to share it.

From the lake, the PCT ascends a couple of switchbacks then rises past the east bank of Susan Jane as it climbs to a narrow pass. Pass a couple of unnamed ponds and, a little more than 1 mile from the lake, reach the junction with Icicle Creek Trail 1551. Turn north and head up to a small, grassy bench dotted with pools.

The trail descends steeply from here to the emerald green waters of Josephine Lake and the perfect spot to enjoy a leisurely lunch if you are just out for the day. This is also a popular place for backpackers looking for a quick escape from the hustle and bustle of the city. The shoreline was once almost loved to death, so respect areas that are being restored and camp only in designated sites.

If you are continuing to Chain Lakes, cross the outlet stream, which is the headwaters of Icicle Creek, and descend a couple switchbacks. From here the trail begins a 2-mile brushy descent down the Icicle Creek drainage. In 0.6 miles the trail reaches the junction with White Pine Trail 1582. Continue following Icicle Creek down the valley, and in 1.5 miles the trail cross the creek on logs and rocks. Just beyond the crossing there is a nice little camp that would break up the hike but avoid the crowds at Josephine Lake.

A quarter mile past the campsite is the turnoff for Chain Lake Trail 1569. Head east up this trail and get ready to do some serious climbing. Steep, tight, rugged switchbacks characterize the start of this 2,000-foot climb to the lake, after which you encounter a seemingly never-ending uphill hike, on which the phrase, "Am I there yet?" may run through your head.

In 2.5 miles (elevation 5,628 feet) you are finally there, and trust me when I say it's worth the effort. The trail arrives at the first of the three lakes and runs along its long, narrow southern shoreline. The valley broadens as you approach the second lake and the true magic of this place is revealed. The lakes rest in a horseshoe basin of craggy ridgelines whose lower slopes are littered with fields of white granite boulders. Parkland meadows brim with flowers and tiny creeks trickle from the snowy slopes. There is great camping, but remember, this area is fragile: Camp only at designated sites or in areas that have already been used.

Once you are settled in, consider an after-dinner hike to Doelle Lakes. To get there, cross the stream between the first and second lakes, and, when the trail forks, take the left branch. The trail rises quickly through talus and offers great views back toward all three lakes. In a little less than 1 mile, the trail reaches a small stand of trees, makes a couple of switchbacks, and rises through a notch in Bulls Tooth Ridge.

Views to the northeast allow you to see just how different the east side of the crest can be. The landscape changes drastically from lush, thick forests to open, much drier slopes. Motivated hikers can descend a few hundred feet through heather to the north shore of the upper lake. Those who feel they have hiked enough can simply retrace their steps to camp and head home.

Hikers looking for a true adventure can make a loop—but only if you have experience with cross-country travel and route finding. Continue east from lower Doelle Lake to Trail 1570, which is no longer maintained. This often hard to find trail travels east then southeast to Frosty Pass. From there you can take Wildhorse Creek Trail 1592 north to Whitepine Creek Trail 1582. Follow this desolate trail back to Icicle Creek and retrace your route north to Stevens Pass.

A bird's-eye view of Doelle Lake

CENTRAL

WHITE PASS TO STEVENS PASS

DIRECTIONS   Drive US 2 to the summit of Stevens Pass. Turn south and follow the signs for the southbound PCT trailhead, which is in the far, eastern lot (parking lot E).

PERMIT   Northwest Forest Pass required. Self-issued permits available at trailhead.

GPS Trailhead Coordinates	20 Chain and Doelle Lakes
UTM Zone (WGS 84)	10T
Easting	0643306
Northing	5289911
Latitude	N47.746642°
Longitude	W121.088206°

CANADA

NORTH CASCADES
NATIONAL PARK

PASAYTEN
WILDERNESS

MT. BAKER-SNOQUALMIE
NATIONAL FOREST

Ross Lake

Pacific Crest Trail

Diablo

OKANOGAN
NATIONAL FOREST

20

Skagit River

Granite Creek

30
29

Mazama

20

Eldorado
Peak

Gardner
Mtn.

20

Marblemount

Cascade River

Mt. Logan

28
27

Twisp River

Stehekin River

LAKE CHELAN
SAWTOOTH
WILDERNESS

20

Pacific Crest Trail

26

GLACIER PEAK
WILDERNESS

Stehekin

Duckbill
Mtn.

Suiattle River

Bonanza
Peak

White Chuck River

25

Mt. Fernow

Lucerne

Pacific Crest Trail Detour

Glacier
Peak

24

23

Lake Chelan

153

HENRY M.
JACKSON
WILDERNESS

White River

Chiwawa River

N. Fork Skykomish River

Entiat River

22

Little Wenatchee River

Lake
Wenatchee

Stormy
Mtn.

Chelan

Skykomish

2

Merritt

97

Stevens
Pass

21

2

S. Fork Skykomish River

ALPINE LAKES
WILDERNESS

WENATCHEE
NATIONAL FOREST

97

Pacific Crest Trail

Icicle Creek

2

Mt.
Daniel

Leavenworth

97

3

NORTH

Stevens Pass to
Canadian Border

21 Lake Valhalla *(page 144)*

22 Cady Ridge to Kodak Peak *(page 149)*

23 Little Giant Pass *(page 155)*

24 Buck Creek Pass *(page 161)*

25 Lyman Lake and Suiattle Pass *(page 167)*

26 Agnes Creek *(page 173)*

27 Rainbow Lake and McAlester Creek *(page 180)*

28 Cutthroat Pass *(page 188)*

29 Grasshopper Pass *(page 193)*

30 Tamarack Peak *(page 198)*

21 Lake Valhalla

SCENERY: ✿ ✿ ✿ ✿
TRAIL CONDITION: ✿ ✿ ✿ ✿
CHILDREN: ✿ ✿ ✿ ✿
DIFFICULTY: ✿ ✿ ✿
SOLITUDE: ✿ ✿

DISTANCE: *8.5 miles (5.5 miles to lake)*
HIKING TIME: *4 hours*
GREEN TRAILS MAP: Benchmark Mountain 144
OUTSTANDING FEATURES: *Alpine lake with good fishing, easy access for an overnight hike with children, and great meadows*

This route's versatility makes it a great option if weather, time, or hiking partners change. A car shuttle is required for the approach I describe; however, you can hike out-and-back from the Stevens Pass or Smithbrook trailheads.

From the rugged terrain of Stevens Pass, the trail starts on an old slightly inclining maintenance road that parallels the highway for about the first 1.5 miles. Stunning views to the east, diverse wildflowers, and occasional glimpses into the quaint neighborhood of Yodelin should distract you from the highway noise.

After a couple miles, the trail begins to wrap around the north-facing slopes of Skyline Ridge as it heads west up the Nason Creek drainage. At this point you cross over the abandoned east entrance of the Cascade Tunnel, part of the Great Northern Railroad (GNR). By far the most rugged section of the GNR, a series of tunnels was built in the Stevens Pass corridor between 1897 and 1929 to protect the trains from the constant avalanches cascading from the slopes above. The worst avalanche fatality in the U.S. occurred at the west entrance of the tunnel, where 96 people on their way from Leavenworth to Seattle were buried in a slide while waiting for weather conditions to improve. Clear-cutting and forest fires started by steam-locomotive sparks were a major cause of the slope's instability.

From here the trail begins a slightly steeper ascent. Your first rewarding view of Lichtenberg Mountain is at 2.3 miles as you enter

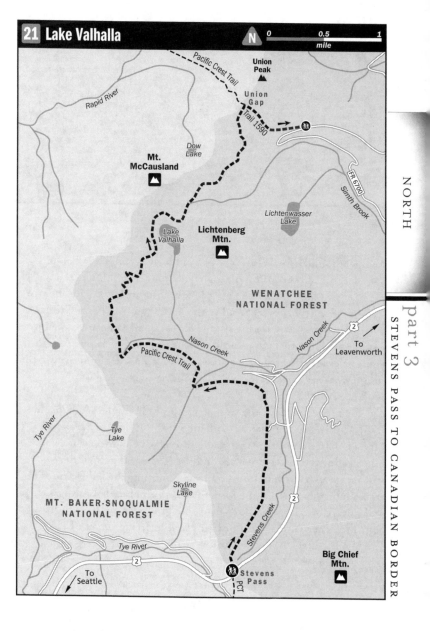

Union Peak

Pacific Crest Trail

Union Gap Trail 1590

Rapid River

Dow Lake

Mt. McCausland

Lake Valhalla

Lichtenberg Mtn.

Lichtenwasser Lake

Smith Brook

FR 6700

WENATCHEE NATIONAL FOREST

Nason Creek

Nason Creek

To Leavenworth

Pacific Crest Trail

Tye River

Tye Lake

Skyline Lake

Stevens Creek

Big Chief Mtn.

MT. BAKER-SNOQUALMIE NATIONAL FOREST

Tye River

To Seattle

Stevens Pass

PCT

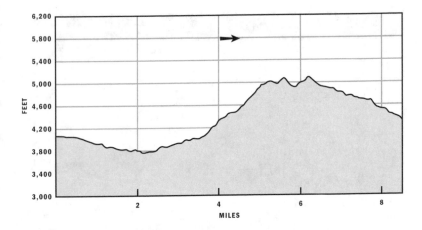

an open boulder field. Just before you hit the 3-mile mark, you'll
see a large, flat rock off on the right side of the trail, the perfect
perch for a water break. The rock is conveniently located just before
a series of switchbacks that lead to the headwaters of Nason Creek. As
you enter the basin, take the spur trail to a small campsite tucked in
a stand of alpine fir atop a knoll. This is a great spot to pitch a tent if
you are looking for a short excursion away from the crowds. Since the
mosquitoes are thick in this area, an outing in late August or Sep-
tember might be your best bet.

From the meadow, the trail begins a steady climb as it gains the
last 1,500 feet to the lake. A flat bench at the 4-mile mark creates a
bit of a "false summit" as the gradient levels out and you can't help
but imagine the lake is "just around the corner." The view here is
still spectacular, with fields of buttercups dotting the landscape. The
trail climbs a forested slope for another mile before rounding a ridge
and traversing a large boulder field with great views to the south and
east. From here it is a short distance to your first glimpse of Lake
Valhalla's crystal-clear waters in the shadow of Lichtenberg's imposing west face.

146

The trail descends to another meadow that is tempting to camp in; however, restoration efforts are under way and you must camp in designated sites on the lakeshore. If you are planning to camp at the lake or are looking for a good place to stop for lunch, continue on the spur trail that descends southeast to reach the northwest shores of the lake. It is worth hiking down there to see the schools of trout swimming up and around the lake's inlet. This is a popular place with day hikers, dog walkers, fisherman, and backpackers on weekends, so be prepared to share this beautiful location.

If you plan to continue to the Smithbrook Trailhead, hike back to the junction and head east on the Pacific Coast Trail (PCT). Along the way you will get a breathtaking view of the lake with the snow-capped mountains of the Chiwakum range in the background. Even if you are not doing this as a thru-hike, it is well worth the effort to hike up to this vantage point.

Approximately 0.5 miles from the junction, you reach a saddle where snow can linger until late July. Use caution when descending from the saddle even if it is sunny and warm. As the trail descends to the northeast, Lichtenberg changes form once again as steep creeks pour over large granite slabs to make their way into the gurgling waters of Smith Brook.

The trail meanders along, views come and go, and the number of people seems to increase. It is now obvious where the majority of hikers came from, as it is only 3 miles to the lake from the Smithbrook Trailhead. However, the climb is much steeper, gaining 800 feet in the first 0.8 miles. At 2.2 miles you reach a junction. The PCT continues north toward Union Gap while the Smithbrook Trail makes its steep descent to Forest Road 6700. If your feet need a pick-me-up before the drive back home, take a minute to soak them in Smithbrook's healing waters.

DIRECTIONS TO STEVENS PASS TRAILHEAD: Drive US 2 to the summit of Stevens Pass. Continue to the second parking lot on the north side of the highway. The trailhead is behind the electric power substation in the far right corner of the parking lot.

TO SMITHBROOK ROAD 6700 TRAILHEAD: From Stevens Pass, continue east on US 2 and turn left onto Smithbrook Road 6700, approximately 0.6 miles from milepost 68. Follow the gravel road 3.1 miles to the Smithbrook Trailhead, on the left side of the road.

PERMIT Northwest Forest Pass required. Self-issued permits available at trailhead.

GPS Trailhead Coordinates	21 Lake Valhalla
UTM Zone (WGS 84)	10T
Easting	0643306
Northing	5289911
Latitude	N47.746642°
Longitude	W121.088206°

SCENERY: ☖ ☖ ☖ ☖ ☖	HIKING TIME: *2–3 days*
TRAIL CONDITION: ☖ ☖ ☖	GREEN TRAILS MAP: Benchmark
CHILDREN: ☖	Mountain 144
DIFFICULTY: ☖ ☖ ☖ ☖	OUTSTANDING FEATURES: *Alpine ridge walks*
SOLITUDE: ☖ ☖ ☖	*with sweeping views into Glacier Peak Wilderness, a*
DISTANCE: *18 miles*	*variety of backpacking loops, great wildflowers, and*
	abundant wildlife

If you find yourself with a bundle of vacation days, I strongly suggest you take them all at once, grab your pack, and head out to this breathtaking area's myriad trails. If you arrive to discover a packed parking lot, don't worry. The endless routes within the first 0.5 miles send people off in all directions.

🏃🏃 Give yourself a few days to explore this amazing area. Plenty of trail systems allow you to access cool routes that can be hiked as extended backpacking loops or as out-and-back day hikes from camp. The route described here ascends Cady Ridge to the PCT and heads north to Kodak Peak, where there are numerous hiking options once you ascend a bit. The many other trails referenced along the way will help you plan an unforgettable trip.

From the lower parking lot, take Cady Creek Trail 1501. The path dips down to the crystal-clear waters of the Little Wenatchee River and crosses it over a large, sturdy bridge. In 0.5 miles you will reach a junction with Cady Creek Trail 1501, which heads west up the brushy banks of Cady Creek to the PCT. Turn north onto Cady Ridge Trail 1532 and begin a series of long, mellow switchbacks through the cool shade of the forest for the next mile or so.

Enjoy this section because, just as the canopy seems to open, the switchbacks get tighter and the tread gets rougher. Although only a mile, this steep, dusty section makes you feel like you are earning every bit of the reward that awaits. Just when you start to wonder if it

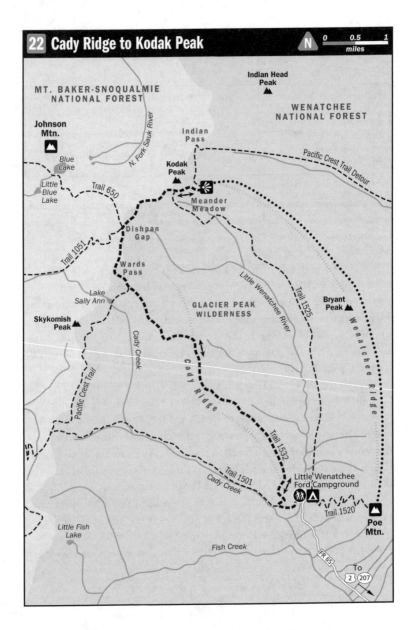

Indian Head
Peak

MT. BAKER-SNOQUALMIE
NATIONAL FOREST

WENATCHEE
NATIONAL FOREST

Johnson
Mtn.

Blue
Lake

Indian
Pass

Pacific Crest Trail Detour

Little
Blue
Lake

Kodak
Peak

Trail 650

Meander
Meadow

Trail 1051

Dishpan
Gap

Wards
Pass

Little Wenatchee River

Trail 1525

Bryant
Peak

Lake
Sally Ann

GLACIER PEAK
WILDERNESS

Skykomish
Peak

Pacific Crest Trail

Cady Creek

Cady Ridge

Wenatchee Ridge

Trail 1532

Trail 1501

Little Wenatchee
Ford Campground

Cady Creek

Trail 1520

Poe
Mtn.

Little Fish
Lake

Fish Creek

FR 65

To
2 207

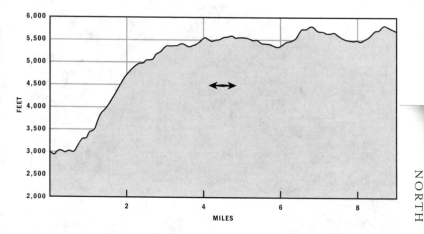

is worth it, the gradient eases and the first of many vistas comes into view. The Wenatchee ridge rises across the valley to the east, its rocky ridgeline formed by the extensions from Longfellow Mountain and Bryant Peak.

From here the trail wanders in and out of forests and meadows, alternating from the east side to the west side of the ridge, with a few sections actually traveling along the ridge itself until it reaches a high point at 5,600 feet. If you were impressed with the views to here, you will feel downright giddy as you descend from the high point onto the broad, open slopes of upper Cady Ridge. Views open in just about every direction as the trail makes a steady descent along the west side of the ridge. Grassy knolls between fields of low-lying huckleberry bushes provide the perfect perch for those wanting to take a load off to rest tired feet and sore legs.

Press on as the trail gradually descends, losing 200 feet in a little less than 1 mile. As it begins to flatten out, there is a nice camp nestled in a patch of alpine firs with a great view of Glacier Peak and Meander Meadow. This is a good choice if you want to avoid

A sign for the PCT marks the turnoff for Kodak Peak.

the crowds that tend to gather on and around the PCT. There is no water source here, but Lake Sally Ann is a little more than 0.5 miles away—you will want to check it out anyway.

From the camp, the trail makes a steep, short climb to the PCT (note that Cady Ridge Trail is not signed here). There are a couple of options from this point. Heading south along the PCT, in 0.5 miles you arrive at Lake Sally Ann, its calm, greenish-blue waters contrasting sharply with the grey and black hues of the rocky crags that rise steeply above. This spot is a must-see, and a dip in the chilly water is a must-do after the steep, dusty climb it took to get here. The lake has ample camping, but fires are prohibited. You can make a loop hike from here by continuing south to Cady Pass and heading out Cady Creek Trail 1501, for a round-trip hike of about 16 miles.

To continue to Kodak Peak from the junction, head north along the PCT. The trail soon crosses a small stream before winding its way up switchbacks to bring you to Wards Pass. Once again you will be awe-inspired, as you look west at Monte Cristo, a monstrous mound of jagged rock and snowbound slopes.

From the pass, hike around the west side of Point 5905. As you approach a small saddle on the north side of the point, you get a great view of Kodak Peak's knobby summit. In another mile you reach Dishpan Gap, a four-way junction affording even more opportunities to check out this magical area. If you want to explore some of the drainages, head down the Skykomish River (1051), up Pass Creek (1053) to Cady Pass, and out Cady Creek back to the Little Wenatchee Ford Campground. This loop's total distance is about 23 miles.

You can also make a quick trip to the rockbound waters of Blue Lake northwest of Dishpan Gap. Diehard loop hikers can continue south from the lake to Little Blue Lake and hike back to Dishpan Gap on Trail 650, adding a little more than 5 miles to the hike. For those continuing along the PCT, drop northeast around a bowl containing a couple of feeder streams that eventually join the Little Wenatchee. As the trail begins to head east, two rock pyramids seem to jut up out of nowhere. Side by side, these two unnamed features provide a striking contrast to the broad ridgelines and lush meadows that dominate most of this area.

These two rock formations become visible as you approach Little Wenatchee River Trail and Meander Meadow. The majority of overnighters in this area head out this trail for a pleasant one- or two-night backpacking trip. If you are feeling more adventurous, follow the PCT as it makes its way around Kodak Peak, through meadows of cotton

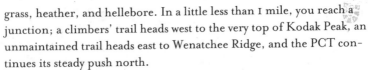

grass, heather, and hellebore. In a little less than 1 mile, you reach a junction; a climbers' trail heads west to the very top of Kodak Peak, an unmaintained trail heads east to Wenatchee Ridge, and the PCT continues its steady push north.

If you are looking for solitude and adventure, hike out the Wenatchee Ridge—no trails, no people, and no water by midsummer combine to create an unforgettable experience. This route is recommended only for experienced backpackers prepared to do some seriously traversing and ridgeline route-finding over rugged terrain rarely traveled by anyone other than hunters enjoying the high hunt in the fall. The ridge eventually joins Poe Mountain Trail 1520, which descends steeply, losing 3,000 feet in 2.5 miles on its way down to Little Wenatchee Trail. When you reach this junction, turn south to reach the parking lot in about 0.25 miles.

DIRECTIONS Take US 2 east 19 miles of Stevens Pass. Turn left (north) onto WA 207 toward Lake Wenatchee. Cross the Wenatchee River and take the left fork. Continue on this road until it reaches another fork, and take the left branch across some open fields and over the White River. Follow FR 65 (which eventually turns into FR 6500) for about 15 miles, until it ends at Little Wenatchee Ford Campground.

PERMIT Northwest Forest Pass required. Sign in at trailhead.

GPS Trailhead Coordinates	22 Cady Ridge to Kodak Peak
UTM Zone (WGS 84)	10T
Easting	0661924
Northing	5321431
Latitude	N47.917310°
Longitude	W121.087519°

23 Little Giant Pass

SCENERY: ✿ ✿ ✿ ✿ ✿
TRAIL CONDITION: ✿ ✿
CHILDREN: ✿
DIFFICULTY: ✿ ✿ ✿ ✿
SOLITUDE: ✿ ✿ ✿ ✿
DISTANCE: 10 miles

HIKING TIME: 6–8 hours
GREEN TRAILS MAP: Holden 113
OUTSTANDING FEATURES: A magnificent view into the enchanting Napeequa Valley, a chilly river crossing to get the adrenalin pumping, and a some-what grueling climb that earns you a hearty dinner at the end of the day

This section of trail is part of the PCT reroute created in 2003 after sections of the PCT were destroyed by severe flooding. This stretch is now considered one of the hardest because of the steep, rugged terrain and an unavoidable river crossing. A number of PCT hikers bypass this section and, unfortunately, miss out on some the most breathtaking scenery the PCT has to offer. Don't be intimidated: Take your time and know that the views into the Napeequa Valley are more than worth the effort. It is best to do this hike at the end of season, when the water levels are low and you feel strong after conditioning yourself all summer.

Pulling up to the trailhead, you may wonder where all the other cars are. Well, for starters, the hike begins with a nerve-racking crossing of the Chiwawa River, which early in the season can turn back even the most adventurous of spirits. Secondly, it is a lung-burner on the way up and a knee-pounder on the way down, gaining 4,000 feet in a little more than 4.5 miles. Lastly, on a warm summer day, sections of the trail can cook, and on a rainy day it turns into a muddy, rutted-out mess.

So, why would you even consider tackling this hike? There are numerous reasons, but solitude, incredible views that will literally take your breath away, and bright green, grassy meadows splashed with a colorful assortment of wildflowers are my favorites.

To begin, follow the trail west a short way to the Chiwawa River ford (elevation 2,600 feet). By late in the season, it is possible to wade

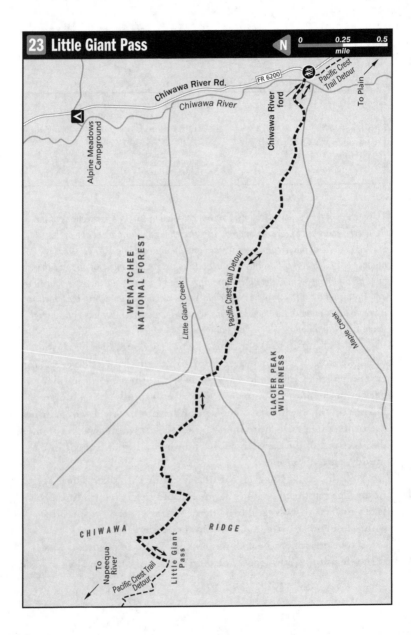

N

0   0.25   0.5
mile

Chiwawa River Rd.   FR 6200

Pacific Crest Trail Detour

Chiwawa River

To Plain

Alpine Meadows Campground

Chiwawa River ford

WENATCHEE NATIONAL FOREST

Little Giant Creek

Pacific Crest Trail Detour

Chiwawa River

Maple Creek

GLACIER PEAK WILDERNESS

CHIWAWA   RIDGE

To Napeequa River

Pacific Crest Trail Detour

Little Giant Pass

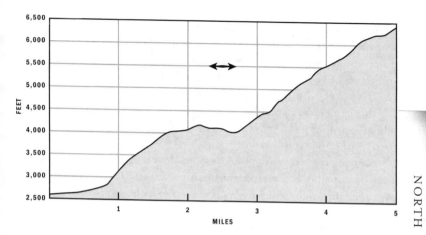

across this frigid river; in any case, be prepared to get wet. If the river looks high, it may be worth spending a little extra time in search of a logjam to scamper across. If neither wading nor scampering is feasible, save this hike for another day. Fortunately, there are a number of wonderful hikes (including Buck Creek) farther down the road.

Once you safely cross the river, the trail can be tricky to find. Locate the most well-traveled path and follow it along the overgrown roads that were once a part of Maple Creek Campground. In 0.25 miles the trail crosses Maple Creek on another somewhat confusing maze of trails. Pick up the main trail on the north side of the creek and follow it as it parallels the creek a short way.

Enjoy leisurely switchbacks that wind back and forth through stands of pine trees for the next mile or so. After this you face a steep, grueling climb to a saddle. While catching your breath, take a look around at the stands of dying trees, a sign of the elusive pine bark beetle that has affected hundreds of thousands of acres in the Cascade Range.

Bark beetles are a part of the natural environment, and in a healthy forest they contribute by creating habitats for other animals and assist in fire ecology, a vital component for pine forests in particular. Forests affected by years of drought, poor management practices, and fire suppression are much more susceptible to massive outbreaks of beetles, which burrow into the bark, gradually killing the trees from within. Many land management agencies are studying this epidemic in an effort to mitigate large-scale occurrences and reduce the risk of catastrophic fires that can rip through these patches of standing dead timber.

Leaving the saddle, the trail descends to a crossing of the South Fork of Little Giant Creek (elevation 4,000 feet). The few campsites on either side of the creek have a tendency to be buggy during the summer months.

After crossing the creek, avoid a trail that branches north through a grassy meadow. Follow the trail that turns upstream, paralleling the creek.

Take a breath because now it's time to climb. From here the trail gains 2,400 feet in 2.5 miles. On the bright side, views continually open as you climb ever higher into the alpine. A quarter mile from the creek crossing, you enter a stand of burnt timber, remnants from the Maple Creek fire that burned 2,300 acres back in the summer of 2003. New life is beginning to appear, and if your timing is right, you'll find fireweed covering the forest, its bright pink flower creating a dramatic contrast to the charcoal snags that surround it.

Continue to climb as the trail becomes steep, narrow, and extremely rutted in places. This stretch evidences nothing like the caliber of trail maintenance many PCT thru-hikers come to expect, which is why some of the less hardy ones avoid this section altogether.

Around 3 miles the trail cuts through a broad ridge composed of schist, and views into Little Giant Creek to the north and Maple Creek to the south offer a welcome distraction from the pain in your legs. The trail is a bit brushy in places, but in another mile it transitions into lush meadows carpeted with wildflowers. A long traverse eventually brings you to a notch in the middle of Chiwawa Ridge known as Little Giant Pass (elevation 6,400 feet).

The views from here will literally take your breath away. The milky blue water of the Napeequa River snakes its way through the valley far below, and cascading waterfalls tumble from all sides through a patchwork of greenery. Clark Mountain's shimmering slopes are the most prominent feature to the west and, on a clear day, Glacier Peak is visible just beyond the head of the valley. For even more stunning views, take a walk up either of two knolls, one north and one south of the pass.

If the views from here just aren't enough, an unmaintained trail drops steeply from the pass down to the valley floor (elevation 4,400 feet). A warning before you go scurrying off: The trail resembles more of a sheep trail than a hiking trail and is barely visible at times. This route is suitable only for experienced hikers—and, remember, what goes down, must come up. You can camp on gravel bars along the river if you need to.

If you've had enough for one day, simply reverse your route. You'll quickly learn why so many PCT hikers curse this section. At least the time goes by fast. Soon you'll be back at the Chiwawa River crossing. Unlike the first time through, the second time feels so good to your tired legs that you can almost hear them say "Ahhhh" when they hit the ice-cold water. Enjoy the moment before heading to the far bank and returning to your car.

DIRECTIONS   From Stevens Pass, head east on US 2 to WA 207 (the turnoff for Lake Wenatchee). Turn left and follow the road over the Wenatchee River, veering right at the fork just after the bridge onto Chi-wawa Loop Road. Follow it 1.4 miles and turn left onto Chiwawa River Road (FR 6200). Drive 19 miles to the trailhead on the left side of the road. There is a shoulder for a few cars to park.

GPS Trailhead Coordinates	23 Little Giant Pass
UTM Zone (WGS 84)	10U
Easting	0660126
Northing	5326618
Latitude	N48.025626°
Longitude	W120.828170°

24 Buck Creek Pass

SCENERY: 🐾 🐾 🐾 🐾 🐾
TRAIL CONDITION: 🐾 🐾 🐾 🐾
CHILDREN: 🐾 🐾
DIFFICULTY: 🐾 🐾 🐾
SOLITUDE: 🐾 🐾
DISTANCE: *19 miles*

HIKING TIME: *2–3 days*
GREEN TRAILS MAP: Holden 113
OUTSTANDING FEATURES: *Fields and fields of wildflowers, a bit of Washington history, and great alpine day hikes from camp*

This leg of the PCT is part of a reroute created in 2003 after floods devastated Glacier Peak Wilderness, taking out roads, bridges, and trails, including large sections of the PCT. Estimates vary as to when and if the original route will be fixed, but until then, I'm sure PCT thru-hikers will be anything but disappointed with this beautiful stretch through Buck Creek.

🏃 This hike begins on an abandoned road now heavily used by equestrians, hikers, hunters, and climbers. In the late 1800s this was also a popular route for sheepherders, who grazed livestock in the high, lush meadows throughout the summer. Their route, known as the Rock Creek Allotment, covered more than 50 miles of rough terrain that began farther east up the Rock Creek drainage, where the weather was drier and the snow disappeared more quickly. By late summer or early fall, the flocks would arrive at Buck Creek Pass and from there begin a slow descent out Buck Creek, grazing along the way.

Before the Forest Service was established in 1908, these high alpine meadows were open to all. By the 1930s the Forest Service had begun regulating the area to prevent further damage to the meadows and reduce soil erosion. The number of sheep allowed in certain areas was drastically limited, and designated grazing sites were established.

As you hike along the lower portion of the trail, sections of the sheepherding route can supposedly still be seen through the trees, but I never saw it. The upper section of the trail was rerouted high above the bright-green grazing meadows because the route along

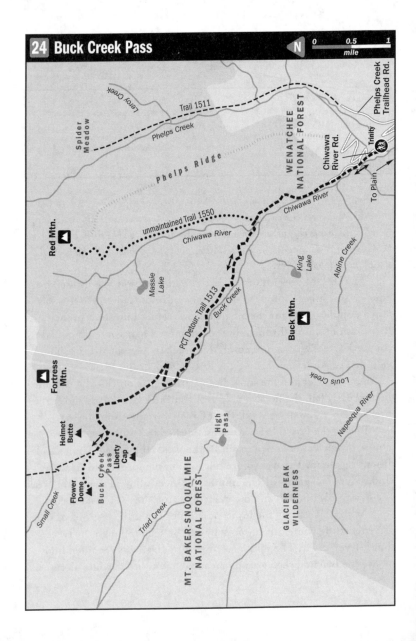

0   0.5   1
mile

Phelps Creek Trailhead Rd.

Leroy Creek

Trail 1511

Spider Meadow

Phelps Creek

WENATCHEE NATIONAL FOREST

Chiwawa River Rd.

Trinity

Phelps Ridge

To Plain

Chiwawa River

unmaintained Trail 1550

Red Mtn.

Chiwawa River

King Lake

Alpine Creek

Massie Lake

Buck Creek

PCT Detour: Trail 1513

Buck Mtn.

Fortress Mtn.

Louis Creek

Helmet Butte

Napeequa River

Flower Dome

Buck Creek Pass

Liberty Cap

High Pass

GLACIER PEAK WILDERNESS

Small Creek

Triad Creek

MT. BAKER-SNOQUALMIE NATIONAL FOREST

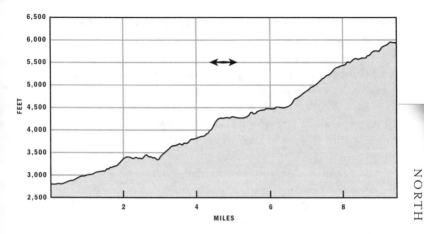

Buck Creek was steep and difficult to follow. Even though this area is no longer used for grazing, take a moment to appreciate the hard work the sheep and their herders put in to establish this beloved route that is used by so many people today.

Leaving the trailhead (elevation 2,770 feet), cross Phelps Creek on a large bridge just above the confluence with the Chiwawa River. From here Phelps Creek branches to the northeast and you begin an ascent up the Chiwawa River drainage. In a little more than 0.25 miles, the trail skirts the old mining town of Trinity, another piece of this area's rich history. The Royal Development Company established the town in 1918 after prospectors discovered traces of copper ore in the area. The mine was closed in the 1930s and is owned by a private resident. Electricity for the small site is still generated by a power plant due west of town on the Chiwawa River.

One mile from the trailhead, you enter Glacier Peak Wilderness. In another 0.5 miles the trail splits. The right trail climbs to the head of the Chiwawa River and the site of an old mine on Red Mountain. Take the left branch along Trail 1513 and follow it 1.75

miles to a crossing of the Chiwawa River. Just beyond the bridge is a large forested campsite.

You now begin an ascent up the Buck Creek drainage. The trail climbs switchbacks to top out on a bench, where great views open to the west toward the daunting slopes of Buck Mountain (elevation 8,538 feet). At 4.5 miles the trail passes through the first of many parkland meadows that lie at the base of enormous avalanche paths. Be sure to keep an eye out for faint traces of the old sheep trail.

At around 5 miles you are rewarded with sweeping views of the entire valley. Looking ahead, Buck Mountain's hanging glaciers, permanent snowfields, and towering cliffs contrast starkly with the brilliant-green avalanche swaths that descend to the valley floor. A number of unnamed peaks extend beyond Buck Mountain toward High Pass, a place of rugged beauty few are privileged to see.

In 0.5 miles the trail reaches a forested camp beside a small creek. This site would do in a pinch, but it is right next to the trail, affording little privacy. The next site is another 0.5 miles down the trail and is much larger, has great views, and sits a little farther back from the trail. It looks like horsepackers use it a lot, but there are a couple of small hiker sites on the right side of the trail.

The next section of trail is impressive, passing through a mess of broken trees, snapped in half or blown to pieces by powerful slides that tore down from the west side of the valley. A bit farther on, you pass through remnants of another, much older slide, where hundreds of white, weathered trees lay on the ground like matchsticks.

At 4,500 feet the trail leaves the valley floor, beginning a 1,300-foot climb to Buck Creek Pass. The path heads southeast a short way before it resumes its course up valley. As you wrap around the head of the valley, the mighty Fortress Mountain (elevation 8,674 feet) comes into view to the northeast, and to the south you can see your entire route up the Chiwawa and Buck Creek drainages.

Buck Creek Pass

The trail continues through Buck Creek basin, traversing below the flowery meadows of Helmet Butte and, at 9.5 miles, finally arrives at Buck Creek Pass (elevation 5,787 feet). As you will soon understand, the pass is famous for its amazing wildflowers and jaw-dropping views of Glacier Peak. There is great camping only a couple hundred feet below the trail, in the pass itself.

Exploratory options abound, so the more time you have to spend up here, the better. For a spectacular sunset, walk up the colorful slopes of Flower Dome to catch the alpenglow on Glacier Peak.

If you're looking for a half-day hike from camp, head south 1.5 miles to the top of Liberty Cap (elevation 6,800 feet), where a display of wildflowers, including glacier lilies, lupine, columbine, anemones, and paintbrush, are sure to keep you snapping pictures. The views from here aren't too shabby either, with Glacier Peak's glistening slopes dominating the skyline to the west, Chiwawa and Fortress mountains standing proudly to the northeast, and Buck

Mountain, Chiwawa Ridge, and the White Mountains rising steeply to the south. When you are finished taking it all in, retrace your route to the trailhead.

DIRECTIONS From Stevens Pass, drive east on US 2 to WA 207 (the turnoff for Lake Wenatchee). Turn left and follow the road over the Wenatchee River, veering right at the fork just after the bridge, onto Chiwawa Loop Road. Follow the road 1.4 miles and turn left onto Chiwawa River Road (FR 6200). Continue about 23 miles to the road's end and a large parking area, just beyond Phelps Creek Campground.

PERMIT Northwest Forest Pass required. Sign in at trailhead.

GPS Trailhead Coordinates	24 Buck Creek Pass
UTM Zone (WGS 84)	10U
Easting	0664883
Northing	5340857
Latitude	N48.072721°
Longitude	W120.850328°

SCENERY: ✿ ✿ ✿ ✿	DISTANCE: *22 miles out-and-back to the PCT,*
TRAIL CONDITION: ✿ ✿ ✿	*38 miles to Stehekin Road*
CHILDREN: ✿ ✿ ✿	HIKING TIME: *2–5 days*
DIFFICULTY: ✿ ✿ ✿	GREEN TRAILS MAP: Holden 113
SOLITUDE: ✿ ✿ ✿	OUTSTANDING FEATURES: *Cascading waterfalls, turquoise-blue lakes, glaciers, and colorful alpine meadows*

This trail barely intersects the PCT, but it was too good to leave out. You could continue out Agnes Creek along the PCT. If you don't have time to do it as a thru-hike, an overnight to Lyman Lake is just as spectacular, and there is plenty to explore from camp. If you are looking for a shorter hike or have children with you, Hart Lake is only 4 miles from Holden Village and is a great, though popular, option.

The trail begins from the remote Lutheran village of Holden. Exploration of this area began back in 1877, when railroad companies sent surveyors to find a route through the Central Cascades. Obviously, they didn't find one, but their journey led to an influx of prospectors in search of mining claims.

In 1896, after years of roaming the hills and valleys around Lake Chelan, James Henry Holden staked his first claim. Unfortunately, Holden would not live to see a working mine as it would be another 42 years and nearly $3 million worth of investments before the first shipment of copper, gold, and zinc concentrate would make it into production. The mine prospered from 1938 to 1957, producing $100 million in metals. After World War II the price of metal dropped; nearly all of the resources had been extracted, forcing the mine to shut down in 1957.

The Howe Sound Company bought the business in 1928, salvaging most of the mining equipment. It tried to sell the village for $100,000. In the end, a persistent buyer from the Lutheran Bible Institute (known today as Trinity Lutheran College), named Wes

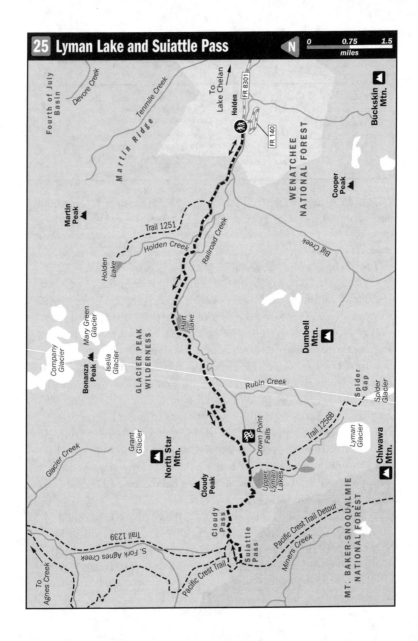

N

0   0.75   1.5
miles

Fourth of July Basin

Devore Creek

Tenmile Creek

To Lake Chelan

FR 8301

Buckskin Mtn.

Holden

FR 140

M a r t i n   R i d g e

WENATCHEE NATIONAL FOREST

Cooper Peak

Martin Peak

Trail 1251

Holden Creek

Railroad Creek

Holden Lake

Big Creek

GLACIER PEAK WILDERNESS

Mary Green Glacier

Company Glacier

Bonanza Peak

Isella Glacier

Hart Lake

Dumbell Mtn.

Rubin Creek

Spider Gap

Grant Glacier

Glacier Creek

North Star Mtn.

Crown Point Falls

Trail 1256B

Spider Glacier

Lyman Glacier

Cloudy Peak

Upper Lyman Lakes

Chiwawa Mtn.

To Agnes Creek

Trail 1239

S. Fork Agnes Creek

Cloudy Pass

Suiattle Pass

Pacific Crest Trail

Pacific Crest Trail Detour

Miners Creek

MT. BAKER-SNOQUALMIE NATIONAL FOREST

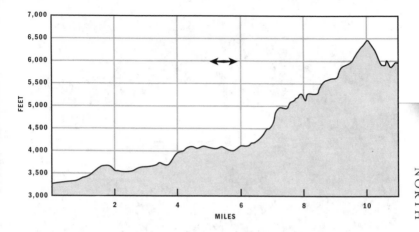

Prieb, bought it for $1. Prieb raised money and brought in volunteers to restore the buildings and eventually turn it into what you see today. The village is open to everyone, so, if time permits, make a reservation to stay a night or two and explore a bit of Washington history.

To get to the trailhead from the village, head west 0.75 miles through town on the main (and only) dirt road, past remnants of the old mining town. From the trailhead, the trail skirts a washed-out section of road and then resumes its course on the dirt road. A 0.25-mile hike brings you to Glacier Peak Wilderness, where the road turns into a well-maintained, heavily used trail.

In a little less than a mile from the trailhead, you reach the turn-off for Holden Lake. This is a popular, yet strenuous day hike for anglers and visitors staying at Holden. Beyond the junction the trail travels along a broad valley bottom with stands of pine, aspen, and cottonwood. Views of North Star open to the west, Dumbell Mountain rises sharply from the Big Creek drainage to the southwest, and Copper Mountain can be seen to the south.

Cross the outlet of Holden Lake on a footbridge around the 2-mile mark; the trail enters the forest for 0.5 miles. You have open

Hiking near upper Lyman Lake

views again as you reach a field filled with grasses, sedges, shrubs, and snags. Railroad Creek moves ever so slowly, parallel to the trail.

This mellow, flat section soon ends, and the gradient steepens as you climb the last 300 feet to Hart Lake (elevation 3,956). The trail tops out 100 feet or so above the shoreline and then descends on the north side of the lake. Tucked among crackling aspens and rustling cottonwoods on the west shoreline, near the lake's inlet are some great campsites. A night here is a nice way to break up the hike if you decide to head out on the same day you catch the shuttle to Holden.

The trail continues up Railroad Creek, crossing it not long after leaving Hart Lake. Waterfalls dominate the scenery for the next mile. Crown Point Falls rumbles loudly up the drainage, and unnamed falls and steep creeks tumble from the lower flanks of mighty Bonanza Peak (elevation 9,511), the highest nonglaciated peak in Washington.

Rebel Camp is 4.8 miles from the trailhead. This site is forested, but views are fairly open and there is a small creek running nearby. If you lack time or energy, this is another good place to stop before the dusty, brushy, 1,500-foot climb. You are rewarded with close-up views of Crown Point Falls 2 miles from Rebel Camp.

A long, southwestward traverse and a few more switchbacks finally bring you to the meadow-bound shores of lower Lyman Lake (elevation 5,598). There are campsites on the northern shore, just as you approach the lake. You'll find additional sites off a spur trail on the west side of the lake that offer stunning views of Bonanza Peak.

If cascading creeks, opaque blue waters, a glacier-carved valley, and breathtaking alpine views interest you, make the 2-mile journey to the upper Lyman Lakes. Evidence of retreating glaciers is right before your eyes as you hike over rocky moraines and circumnavigate tarns created by the ever-shrinking Lyman Glacier. There are great campsites with fantastic views of Chiwawa Mountain at the two upper lakes, but there is limited shelter from the elements.

To continue on to the PCT, head northwest from lower Lyman Lake, hiking about 2 miles to Cloudy Pass (elevation 6,438). Even if you plan to do this hike as an out-and-back, it is worth hiking here for the views alone. The entire Agnes Creek valley stretches to the north, towering peaks and rugged ridges lining either side. A climb up Cloudy Peak wins views of the wild, rugged Glacier Peak.

To do this as a thru-hike to Stehekin, descend steeply to a junction with Suiattle Pass Trail. Take the hikers trail through steep boulders to reach Suiattle Pass. From there, head south on the PCT and follow the trail description for Agnes Creek (Hike 26, page 173).

DIRECTIONS   From Seattle, take US 2 over Stevens Pass about 150 miles, to Wenatchee. Take the exit for 97 Alt toward Rocky Reach Dam and Lake Chelan. The Lady of the Lake Ferry Terminal is on your left as you come into town, just past the sign marking the 30 mile-per-hour speed zone. It is about two hours on *Lady of the Lake II* to Lucerne. Verify pricing and schedules before you head out. From Lucerne, take the Holden shuttle 10 miles to Holden Village. Contact Holden Village to make shuttle reservations and verify times.

If you plan to do this as a through-hike, take the bus from High Bridge Ranger Station (where you'll find schedules posted) to Stehekin. Catch *Lady of the Lake II* or the *Lady Express*, which is more expensive but much faster. Tickets can be purchased ahead of time or with cash or check at the dock.

PERMIT   Sign in at trailhead.

GPS Trailhead Coordinates	25 Lyman Lake and Suiattle Pass
UTM Zone (WGS 84)	10U
Easting	0664883
Northing	5340857
Latitude	N48.199517°
Longitude	W120.781005°

26 Agnes Creek

SCENERY: ☆☆☆☆
TRAIL CONDITION: ☆☆☆
CHILDREN: ☆
DIFFICULTY: ☆☆☆
SOLITUDE: ☆☆☆☆
DISTANCE: *38 miles out and back, 30 miles to Holden Village*

HIKING TIME: *3–5 days*
GREEN TRAILS MAPS: Holden 113 *and* McGregor Mountain 81
OUTSTANDING FEATURES: *Groves of beautiful cedar trees, alpine views, a peaceful boat ride on the third-deepest lake in the nation, and a chance to swing through the Stehekin Bakery*

A four-hour scenic boat ride up Lake Chelan to the small mountain town of Stehekin and an 11-mile bus ride that conveniently stops at the Stehekin Bakery eventually brings you to the trailhead. From there, the trail takes off up a long, remote valley to stunning high country and endless opportunities for exploration. Best of all, you can do this as a thru-hike by exiting through Railroad Creek to the Lutheran-based community of Holden Village, where you'll find showers and accommodation. Another 10-mile shuttle (or hike, if you're feeling really ambitious) brings you back to Lake Chelan.

🚶 To get to the trailhead, take the Stehekin shuttle 11 miles to High Bridge Ranger Station. Cross the bridge and, in about 500 feet, you reach the trailhead, on the left side of the road. Be sure to follow the signs for the southbound PCT, and do not accidentally take Agnes Creek Gorge Trail.

From the trailhead, follow the PCT a short way down to Agnes Creek Gorge. You cross the creek on a wide, sturdy horse bridge that occasionally gets swept away by monster floods or damaged by falling trees. Before heading out, contact Stehekin Ranger Station to verify that the bridge is in place because fording it, even in late summer, is not the safest option.

Once you have crossed the creek, the trail makes its way up long switchbacks. In a little more than a mile, you reach a viewpoint that looks back toward Stehekin Valley and McGregor Mountain. A Park

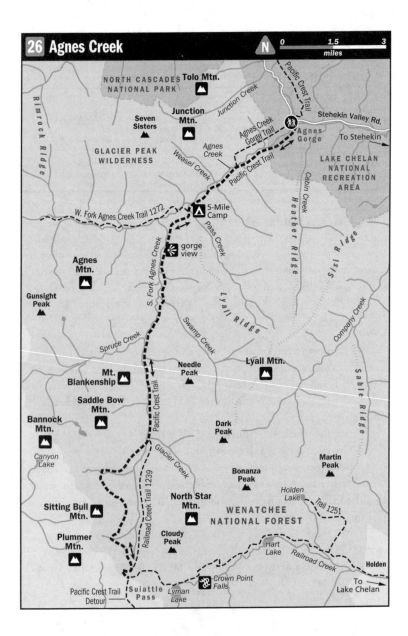

N

0   1.5   3
miles

NORTH CASCADES
NATIONAL PARK

Tolo Mtn.

Junction Creek

Pacific Crest Trail

Stehekin Valley Rd.

Junction
Mtn.

Seven
Sisters

Agnes Creek
Gorge Trail

Agnes
Gorge

To Stehekin

GLACIER PEAK
WILDERNESS

Agnes
Creek

Weasel Creek

Pacific Crest Trail

LAKE CHELAN
NATIONAL
RECREATION
AREA

Rimrock Ridge

W. Fork Agnes Creek Trail 1272

5-Mile
Camp

Cabin Creek

Heather Ridge

Sisi Ridge

S. Fork Agnes Creek

Pass Creek

gorge
view

Agnes
Mtn.

Gunsight
Peak

Lyall Ridge

Company Creek

Spruce Creek

Swamp Creek

Lyall Mtn.

Sable Ridge

Mt.
Blankenship

Needle
Peak

Pacific Crest Trail

Saddle Bow
Mtn.

Bannock
Mtn.

Dark
Peak

Canyon
Lake

Martin
Peak

Glacier Creek

Bonanza
Peak

Railroad Creek Trail 1239

Sitting Bull
Mtn.

North Star
Mtn.

Holden
Lake

Trail 1251

WENATCHEE
NATIONAL FOREST

Holden

Plummer
Mtn.

Cloudy
Peak

Hart
Lake

Railroad Creek

To
Lake Chelan

Pacific Crest Trail
Detour

Suiattle
Pass

Lyman
Lake

Crown Point
Falls

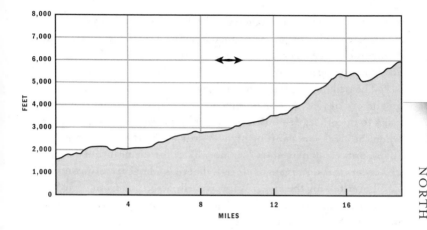

Service radio repeater shimmers in the sun just east of McGregor's summit.

In 0.5 miles the trail exits Lake Chelan National Recreation Area and enters Glacier Peak Wilderness. The trail is fairly dull for the next 3.5 miles as it rolls through forested slopes to the junction with the West Fork of Agnes Creek Trail. This is also the site of 5-Mile Camp, a nice place to stop for the night if you head out on the same day you get dropped off by the ferry. The campsites are located among sparse timber just east of the trail on the west bank of Pass Creek.

Remain on the PCT as you leave 5-Mile Camp, and follow the trail along South Fork Agnes Creek. In 1.4 miles you arrive at a viewpoint that will most likely exhaust your camera's battery. Precarious side trails take off from the main path and teeter on the edge of a deep gorge. Photo opportunities abound and your gaze wanders up from the chaotic torrent toward the hard-to-access, rarely climbed giant known as Agnes Mountain. Beyond Agnes's rocky summit loom the distinctive twin summits of Gunsight Peak.

After taking it all in, continue south on the PCT another 1.6 miles to Swamp Creek Camp. The camp, on the south side of Swamp Creek, is 100 yards or so downstream from the crossing. As you leave the site, you pass a sign for the unmaintained Swamp Creek Trail, which eventually reaches the Dark Glacier on the north side of Dark Peak and is likely a bushwhacking adventure through devil's club and alder.

The walking is pleasant for the next mile or so as the creek slips in and out of view. At one point a massive logjam stretches from one bank to the other, demonstrating just how powerful the water can be when the creeks are running high. A little way farther you arrive at a hiker-only camp named Cedar, most likely for the beautiful western red cedars that dominate the forest. There is a level campsite on a knoll overlooking the creek. Water is easily accessible from camp.

For the next 0.5 miles, the trail parallels the creek. Along the way, it passes through thick forests of red cedar, Douglas fir, hemlock, and spruce, then travels brushy avalanche slopes with open views of Mount Blankenship to the west and Needle Peak to the east.

At just more than 12 miles from the Stehekin Road, the trail arrives at Hemlock Camp, a great site along a tranquil section of the creek. Bear scat was prevalent in this area when I scouted this trip, so be sure to hang your food.

From here the trail splits but eventually rejoins just below Suiattle Pass at South Fork Basin Camp. Railroad Creek Trail, which was the old PCT, heads south up Agnes Creek about 5 miles, through a mix of brushy and forested slopes. You gain elevation gradually, and the scenery is similar to what you have already encountered. This is a good route for those hiking early in the season, when snow may be lingering up high.

The new PCT crosses Agnes Creek and takes a high route to South Fork Basin Camp. This route has a few more ups and downs and is about 1.5 miles longer than Railroad Creek Trail. If you plan to do this as a thru-hike to Holden Village, take the PCT's more challenging but much more rewarding high route.

Remaining on the PCT, cross Agnes on a footbridge and begin a steady 1,000-foot climb. Views to the south, toward Sitting Bull

A marmot basks in the sun.

and North Star, unfold as you work your way into the high country. Approximately 1.5 miles from Hemlock, the trail ascends switchbacks next to a stream that pours steeply over polished slabs of bedrock, a good place to grab some water if you plan to stay at one of the sheltered camps in the Sitting Bull Basin.

The first of those camps is 0.5 miles or so from the creek. This hiker-only camp is tucked into a stand of trees that lie a few hundred yards off the trail. No fires are allowed, and water can be limited.

Continue along the trail as it heads west below Saddle Bow Mountain. Traverse a broad, flower-filled basin, where steep creeks and cascading waterfalls tumble all around. The trail turns south, crosses a creek on a small bridge, and resumes a steady southeast climb to the heathery slopes below Sitting Bull. As the trail levels off, keep an eye out for a couple of designated campsites next to a small stream (elevation 5,400 feet). The views are spectacular, but the sites are exposed, so make sure the weather is decent if you plan to stay up there.

In 0.75 miles the trail passes through a meadow strewn with boulders and clumps of dark, purple gentian. As you continue south,

Descending into Plummer Basin

the trail descends more switchbacks to a second basin, below Plummer Mountain, with a much different character from the first one you entered. Gigantic boulders fill the upper basin, and the trail weaves and winds through these car-sized chunks of rock. As you climb (that's right, get ready for one more push!) back out, Needle Peak and Dark Peak are visible in the distance to the northeast.

A mile from Plummer Basin and nearly 19 miles from the start of your journey, you reach the junction with Railroad Creek Trail 1256. To do this as an out-and-back hike, descend east 0.25 miles into a small basin surrounded by talus slopes of white granite boulders and sheer rock cliffs. This is where you rejoin South Fork Agnes Creek. Descend north, and in 5 miles you arrive back at Hemlock Camp. From there simply retrace your steps to Stehekin Road.

Those interested in hiking to Holden Village, continue south on the PCT to Suiattle Pass. From there head east along a precarious trail to Cloudy Pass. To continue to Holden Village, refer to the trail description for Lyman Lake (Hike 25, page 167).

DIRECTIONS From Seattle, take US 2 over Stevens Pass about 150 miles to Wenatchee. Take the exit for 97 Alt toward Rocky Reach Dam and Lake Chelan. The Lady of the Lake Ferry Terminal is on your left as you come into town, just past the sign marking the 30 mile-per-hour speed zone. There are two ferry options to Stehekin, the *Lady of the Lake II* (4 hours) or the faster, more expensive *Lady Express* (2.5 hours). Verify pricing and schedules before you head out. From Stehekin, take the shuttle to High Bridge Ranger Station.

If you plan to do this as a thru-hike, take the shuttle from Holden Village to the Lucerne boat landing. The ferry will pick you up on its return trip down valley. Contact Holden Village for bus schedules and reservations.

PERMIT None required.

GPS Trailhead Coordinates	26 Agnes Creek
UTM Zone (WGS 84)	10U
Easting	0659974
Northing	5360760
Latitude	N48.379706°
Longitude	W120.839491°

27 Rainbow Lake and McAlester Creek

SCENERY: ✿ ✿ ✿ ✿ ✿	HIKING TIME: *3–5 days*
TRAIL CONDITION: ✿ ✿ ✿	GREEN TRAILS MAPS: McGregor
CHILDREN: ✿ ✿	Mountain 81 *and* Stehekin 82
DIFFICULTY: ✿ ✿ ✿ ✿	OUTSTANDING FEATURES: *Two tranquil*
SOLITUDE: ✿ ✿ ✿	*alpine lakes; vistas of the rugged, glaciated peaks*
DISTANCE: *31.5 miles*	*of the North Cascades; and a long, loop hike into*
	remote and wild country

Unlike many national parks, the North Cascades is not a park you can simply drive through to experience. There is no fancy visitor center to wander through or end-of-the-road extravaganza to snap pictures of. This park's true beauty is revealed only when you venture beyond the pavement and into the heart of the mountains. If you have never experienced the North Cascades, this hike is the perfect opportunity to do just that.

🚶🚶 From the parking area, find the narrow path that takes off from behind the information board in the far, eastern corner of the lot. Then, head south across Highway 20 to pick up the main trail, on the other side of the road. The PCT is not far. Follow it south as it rolls gently through forested slopes 0.8 miles to the junction with Copper Pass/Stiletto Peak Trail. Stay on the PCT Bridge Creek Trail.

Just after the junction, the trail crosses Bridge Creek on a sturdy horse bridge. Beyond the crossing, views open to the east toward the Copper Creek drainage and Stiletto Peak (elevation 7,660 feet). The trail briefly reenters the forest and then crosses another open path at the 2-mile mark. A glance to the west reveals the lower slopes of Frisco Mountain (elevation 7,880 feet) and the huge avalanche paths that stretch down to the valley below. If you hit this trail in early to mid-August, these paths are laden with an assortment of berries, including wild raspberries, thimbleberries, and huckleberries. It's no wonder bears are prevalent in this region.

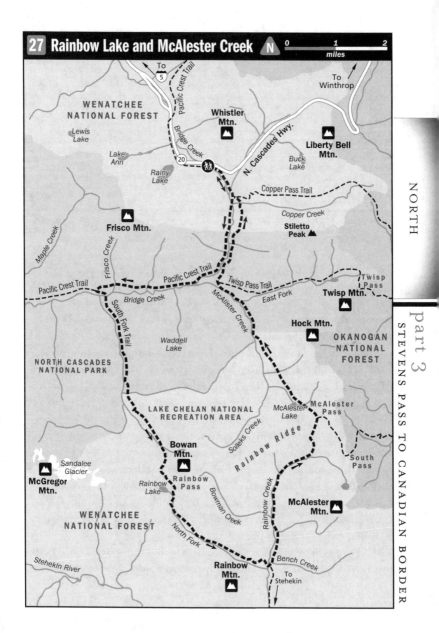

To 5

To Winthrop

WENATCHEE NATIONAL FOREST

Lewis Lake

Lake Ann

Rainy Lake

Whistler Mtn.

Liberty Bell Mtn.

Buck Lake

N. Cascades Hwy.

20

Pacific Crest Trail

Bridge Creek

Copper Pass Trail

Copper Creek

Frisco Mtn.

Stiletto Peak

Frisco Creek

Maple Creek

Pacific Crest Trail

Pacific Crest Trail

Twisp Pass Trail

Twisp Pass

East Fork

Twisp Mtn.

Bridge Creek

South Fork Trail

McAlester Creek

Hock Mtn.

OKANOGAN NATIONAL FOREST

Waddell Lake

NORTH CASCADES NATIONAL PARK

LAKE CHELAN NATIONAL RECREATION AREA

Sollehs Creek

McAlester Lake

McAlester Pass

Rainbow Ridge

South Pass

Sandalee Glacier

McGregor Mtn.

Bowan Mtn.

Rainbow Lake

Rainbow Pass

Bowman Creek

Rainbow Creek

McAlester Mtn.

WENATCHEE NATIONAL FOREST

North Fork

Bench Creek

Stehekin River

Rainbow Mtn.

To Stehekin

NORTH

part 3
STEVENS PASS TO CANADIAN BORDER

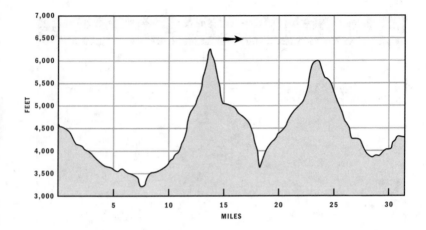

A short distance from here is the Forest Service boundary. Another mile beyond that, the trail makes a slight turn to the west and, at 3.7 miles, arrives at the Twisp Pass junction. If you get a late start on the first day, there is a horse-and-hiker camp called Fireweed 0.1 mile to the east.

To continue toward Rainbow Lake remain on the southbound PCT. The trail turns due west and, at 4.3 miles, the sparkling glaciers of Mount Goode can be seen toward the head of the valley. In another 0.3 miles, the trail reaches Hideaway, a hiker-only camp tucked in a stand of tightly packed trees. The site, beside Bridge Creek, has space for two or three small tents. It is most likely buggy in the summer but is fine if you do not want to share a camp with horses.

Resume hiking on the PCT as the trail wanders in and out of slide paths. The hiking is fairly hot and dusty through this section; however, views south toward McGregor Mountain and the Sandalee Glacier make up for it. At this point, you can also see your route to Rainbow Lake via South Fork Bridge Creek.

At 6.3 miles you reach the junction with South Fork Trail. Take this trail south as it descends steeply toward Bridge Creek. Follow the hiker signs and you soon reach a few large campsites, next to the creek (elevation 3,200 feet). There is no bridge at the crossing, so if you want to do this while the snow is still melting, check with a ranger station to see what conditions are like.

Once you have safely forded Bridge Creek, pick up the trail on the other side and climb steeply 0.5 miles through an old burn. The trail soon reenters the forest, and the gradient eases for the next 2 miles. At the time of this writing, the trail had about a hundred small, downed trees on it, and a ranger I talked to did not give the impression they would be cleared away any time soon. The trees were easy to climb around, but check the latest trail conditions before heading out.

As you slowly work your way up valley, McGregor and Bowan mountains occasionally come into view. At 8.8 miles the trail reaches Dan's Camp, a hiker-only campsite with space for one or two tents— not my first choice, but if South Fork is full or you're looking for solitude, it will work.

At 9 miles you reach Lake Chelan National Recreation Area. Just beyond the boundary, the trail travels 100 yards or so up a meadow to offer a great view of Bowan Mountain.

As you reenter the forest, get ready to climb. See all those squiggle marks on the Green Trails map? That's right, those are tight switchbacks that take you more than 500 feet in 0.5 miles. When the trail reaches 4,800 feet, the incline eases and the north basin of McGregor Mountain comes into full view. The scene is spectacular, with water from the Sandalee Glacier forming creeks that cascade into the valley below.

From this point, the temperature cools as the trail parallels the creek for a stretch through the forest. In 1 mile or so, you reach a beautiful meadow that lies at the base of Bowan Mountain (elevation 7,895 feet). The headwaters of South Fork Bridge Creek tumble down the mountain's rocky flanks before snaking through the meadow, making the trail mucky and fairly hard to follow. If you lose the trail after you cross the creek, look for it to the right of the large boulder field.

You now begin a long ascent through stands of larch, hemlock, and alpine fir. This slope can hold snow well into July and may require an ice axe. After a fairly long, steady climb, the trail eventually tops out at Rainbow Pass (elevation 6,200 feet). Rainbow Lake can be seen 600 feet below in an amphitheater of polished rock walls. Beyond the lake, impressive vistas stretch out to the south toward the two-pronged summit of Tupshin Peak (elevation 8,100 feet) and White Goat Mountain (elevation 7,820 feet). Immediately to the east lies Bowan's summit. Unfortunately, the rock is crumbly and very unappealing to climb. If you are looking to do a little cross-country exploration before you descend to the lake, there is a ridge stretching to the west toward McGregor Mountain that could be worth venturing out on.

To continue to the lake, descend south from the pass until you reach a spur trail that takes you to the eastern shoreline. There are excellent campsites on a bench just above the lake, and in the evening, alpenglow dances on the summits and ridgelines that surround it. There are only four sites and they fill quickly, so try to get a backcountry permit early to secure a place.

From the lake, the trail takes a high route and offers up a panoramic view to the southwest toward the glaciated north face of Dark Peak (elevation 8,504 feet). A series of tiered, rocky, switchbacks descend 500 feet to a forested path. Just before the trail exits the forest and enters the flowery fields of Rainbow Meadows, you see a sign for Rainbow Meadows Group Camp, which offers quick, easy access to the meadow. The Horse Camp is tucked in a stand of trees in another 0.25 miles and the standard sites are at the southern end of the meadow in thick timber, a short distance off the trail.

The next 3 miles travel through a mix of forested and open slopes, offering plenty of opportunities to check out the surrounding

Rainbow Lake and McGregor Mountain

peaks and valleys. Around the 19-mile mark, the trail crosses Rainbow Creek on a foot log and climbs 250 feet to the Rainbow Creek Trail junction. Head north up the Rainbow Creek drainage toward McAlester Pass.

A nice little camp called Bench Creek is just beyond the junction. In another 1.5 miles Bowan Mountain peeks out once again, and in 0.3 miles you arrive at the hiker-only Bowan Camp, which is just off the trail and has year-round water access from Rainbow Creek.

In another mile, the trail boulder-hops across Rainbow Creek once again. From the crossing, the path climbs a couple switchbacks to pop out below Rainbow Ridge. The entire valley stretches to the north and, for the first time, McAlester Pass comes into view.

The next 0.5 miles is fairly flat and remains in the cool shade of the forest. As the trail begins its climb, you get a great opportunity to take photos of McAlester Mountain, at 5,600 feet. One final push brings you to the subalpine meadows of McAlester Pass (elevation 6,000 feet) where exploration opportunities abound. One great option is to hike 1.4 miles to South Pass and wander the high country that extends in either direction.

If you are looking for solitude, there is a one-site, hiker-only camp on the north side of the meadow. Once water dries up in the meadow, though, it is a 0.5-mile walk toward McAlester Lake or Hidden Meadows Horse Camp to get water.

To continue to the lake, head northwest, descending 500 feet in less than 1 mile to a spur trail for McAlester Lake. Follow the hiker signs to find the numerous campsites scattered along the north side of the lake. This is one of the more popular lakes in the area because of the great fishing, easy horse access, and relative proximity to the North Cascades Highway. That said, it is still worth spending a night at this tranquil little lake. If there's no room or you are continuing on, there is a great grassy meadow to eat lunch in just outside the hiker campsites.

Walking is enjoyable for the next 3 miles as you descend into the McAlester Creek drainage. A half mile beyond the national park boundary, the trail crosses the East Fork of McAlester, a potentially hazardous crossing early in the season. In another 0.5 miles you reach the junction with Twisp Pass. Remain on McAlester Creek Trail.

The last campsite on this 30-mile loop is just past the junction. Fireweed Camp is a hiker-and-horse camp on McAlester Creek, the same campsite mentioned earlier as a great place to break up the first or last day of your trip. There are two hiker sites with space for up to 12 people.

From camp, follow the trail as it crosses just below the confluence of McAlester and Bridge creeks. A few hundred feet beyond the crossing, the trail rejoins the PCT. Follow that north 3.7 miles to the start of your hike at the Bridge Creek Trailhead.

DIRECTIONS Take I-5 north to Exit 230 and turn east on WA 20. As you head toward North Cascades National Park, note that there are limited services east of Concrete, so this is your best bet for shopping for food or getting gas. Drive 51 miles past Marblemount to Rainy Pass. Continue east another mile and look for a large parking area, called Bridge Creek, on the north side of the highway. If you are coming from the east, the Bridge Creek Trailhead is about 34 miles from Winthrop, on the north side of the highway.

PERMIT Northwest Forest Pass required. Backcountry permits must be obtained in-person on the first day or up to one day before your backpacking trip on a first-come, first-served basis. Permits are available at the Wilderness Info Center in Marblemount or the USFS ranger stations in Chelan or Winthrop.

GPS Trailhead Coordinates	27 Rainbow Lake and McAlester Creek
UTM Zone (WGS 84)	10U
Easting	0668616
Northing	5374898
Latitude	N48.504554°
Longitude	W120.717175°

28 Cutthroat Pass

SCENERY: ✿ ✿ ✿ ✿ ✿	HIKING TIME: *5–7 hours*
TRAIL CONDITION: ✿ ✿ ✿ ✿ ✿	GREEN TRAILS MAP: Washington Pass 50
CHILDREN: ✿ ✿ ✿	OUTSTANDING FEATURES: *Grand vistas of*
DIFFICULTY: ✿ ✿ ✿	*snowcapped mountains and weather-worn peaks,*
	a gradual ascent on a well-maintained trail, and
SOLITUDE: ✿ ✿	*plenty of opportunities to extend your hike once you*
DISTANCE: *10 miles*	*reach the pass*

While researching the trails for this book, I ran into a gardener from Stehekin who set out to hike the entire PCT in the 1970s. He made it all the way to southern Oregon. When I asked why he didn't keep going, he simply said, "Well, the Pasayten Wilderness was just too beautiful to leave." He hitched a ride back north and hasn't left since. While Cutthroat Pass is not part of Pasayten Wilderness or North Cascades National Park, many believe it should be. Since it's not, however, dog lovers can bring their canine companions.

🚶🚶 Unlike most hikes in the North Cascades, this one begins with a warm-up. The trail is mostly flat for the first 0.25 miles as it travels north through a forest thick with fir, hemlock, and spruce. You hike a few long, leisurely switchbacks before the trail levels out. At the 1-mile mark a rock offers a place to sit and enjoy excellent views to the southwest toward Corteo Peak. Views open to the west as well, but the trail soon reenters the forest, obscuring the vista.

Walking is pleasant as the trail continues its journey north up the Porcupine Creek drainage. At 2 miles, you cross the creek on a footbridge, after which the trail begins a gradual climb to the northeast. In a little less than 1 mile, there is a small campsite beside the trail, a great spot if the weather is bad, but the camping up higher is much more beautiful.

At 3.2 miles, the trail transitions from dark, forested slopes to open meadows littered with wildflowers. Views open in all directions,

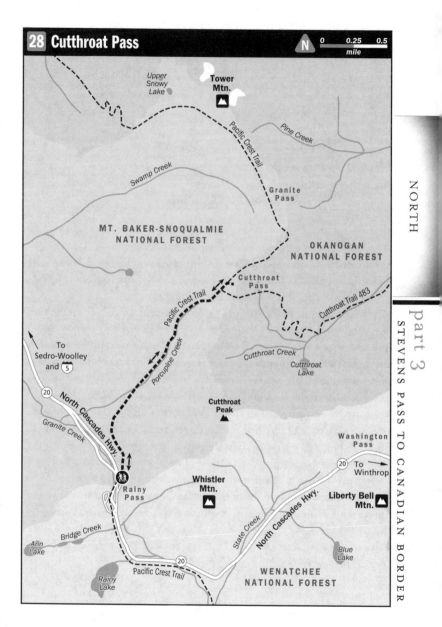

0   0.25   0.5
mile

N

Upper
Snowy
Lake

**Tower
Mtn.**

Pine Creek

Pacific Crest Trail

Swamp Creek

Granite
Pass

**MT. BAKER-SNOQUALMIE
NATIONAL FOREST**

**OKANOGAN
NATIONAL FOREST**

Cutthroat
Pass

Cutthroat Trail 483

Pacific Crest Trail

To
Sedro-Woolley
and (5)

Porcupine Creek

Cutthroat Creek

Cutthroat
Lake

20

North Cascades Hwy.

Granite Creek

**Cutthroat
Peak**

Washington
Pass

20   To
Winthrop

Rainy
Pass

**Whistler
Mtn.**

**Liberty Bell
Mtn.**

North Cascades Hwy.

State Creek

Ann
Lake

Bridge Creek

20

Rainy
Lake

Pacific Crest Trail

**WENATCHEE
NATIONAL FOREST**

Blue
Lake

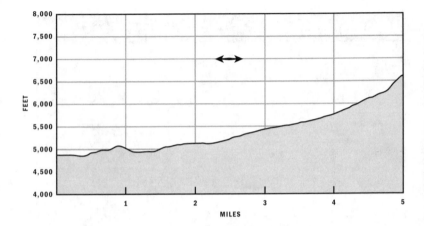

and for the first time you can see Cutthroat Pass at the head of the valley to the northeast. The trail quickly reenters a short section of trees before immersing you in spectacular alpine terrain.

The trail rounds the head of the valley and at 4 miles comes to the best camping in the area. A sign directs hikers to three or four sites that have access to a few small springs, a good place to refill water bottles or let thirsty dogs grab a drink before your final climb to the pass, where water is absent unless snowfields linger.

From here the trail begins a long series of switchbacks. As you wind up the east side of the valley, Peaks 7004 and 7726, to the west, rise steeply above the path you took to get here. The vegetation takes on a scrubbier appearance; harsh winds and fierce storms permit only the strongest of plants to survive. Larch trees, low-lying huckleberry bushes, and heather soon dominate the landscape.

Cutthroat Pass (elevation 6,820 feet) is at 5 miles, and vistas open in all directions. Tower Mountain is directly north, Cutthroat Peak's rocky summit lies to the south, Silver Star dominates views to the east, and the dark-colored rock of Black Peak can be seen to the west.

Cutthroat Peak

And that's just the beginning. If time and energy permit, there is still a ton of exploring to do. Cross-country travelers can venture out on a number of spur trails from the pass. You can also continue another mile north on the PCT to Granite Pass (elevation 6,290 feet), where you will be rewarded once again with breathtaking views of the North Cascades and Pasayten Wilderness.

Not feeling ambitious? Don't worry: There is a large rock, with room for two, conveniently located at the pass for your lounging pleasure. The rock has been worn white from years of use by marmots and mountain folk basking in its warmth in the late afternoon sun.

If you want to spend the night, there are a couple of sites at the pass itself. Be aware that there is no water here once the snow is gone and very limited protection from the elements; storms can roll through without warning. If there is any chance of poor weather, it is probably best to spend the day exploring the pass and the evening hunkered down in the shelter of the campsites you passed on the way up.

To return, simply retrace your steps; or, if you can arrange to swap keys with another hiking party, you can do a thru-hike by descending to Cutthroat Lake via Trail 483. The trail branches off from the PCT just north of Cutthroat Pass; Cutthroat Lake is about 3.5 miles on. From the lake it is another 2 miles to the trailhead.

DIRECTIONS FROM SEATTLE: Take I-5 north to Exit 230 and turn east on WA 20. As you head toward North Cascades National Park, note that there are limited services east of Concrete, so if you need to do any grocery shopping or get gas, this is probably your best bet. Drive 51 miles past Marblemount to Rainy Pass. If you are coming from the east, it is approximately 35 miles from Winthrop. Turn north off of WA 20, following signs for the northbound PCT. The road ends in 0.25 miles, at the trailhead parking lot. The trail is in the back, left (north) corner of the parking lot.

TO CUTTHROAT LAKE TRAIL 483: Continue heading east on WA 20 from Rainy Pass. Turn left (west) about 4.5 miles from Washington Pass, onto Cutthroat Creek Road (Spur Road 400) and drive just more than 1 mile to the road's end. The trailhead is at the end of the road.

PERMIT Northwest Forest Pass required. Sign in at trailhead.

GPS Trailhead Coordinates	28 Cutthroat Pass
UTM Zone (WGS 84)	10U
Easting	0672979
Northing	5380730
Latitude	N48.555789°
Longitude	W120.655731°

29 Grasshopper Pass

SCENERY: ✿ ✿ ✿ ✿

TRAIL CONDITION: ✿ ✿ ✿ ✿ ✿

CHILDREN: ✿ ✿ ✿ ✿

DIFFICULTY: ✿ ✿

SOLITUDE: ✿ ✿

DISTANCE: *11 miles*

HIKING TIME: *4–6 hours*

GREEN TRAILS MAP: Washington Pass 50

OUTSTANDING FEATURES: *Golden larch trees in the fall, abundant wildflowers in the summer, and a 360-degree view of the North Cascades for the entire hike*

This hike's great features should convince you to plan to spend your next vacation in the Methow Valley. For starters, the drive to the trailhead takes you by the Mazama Store, one of my favorite places to stop for a coffee and a berry scone. The Forest Service road is enough beauty for most people, as it steadily climbs through alpine terrain to an elevation of 6,400 feet. Everything beyond the trailhead feels like a bonus as you hike in awe of the grand views surrounding you. The best time to hike it is in fall, when the larches turn a bright, golden yellow. Regardless of when you go, make sure to check the weather before you head out. The trail travels above tree line and offers minimal (if any) protection from nasty weather.

🚶🚶 To begin this hike you can either continue on the main road (5400) past Meadows Campground to Harts Pass and the PCT trailhead—a good option to extend your hike, as it adds 4 miles to an already lengthy day—or you can save some energy to explore the terrain that awaits you by beginning 2 miles south of Harts Pass at Meadows Campground. The trail takes off from the far right corner of the parking lot, and a short, steep pitch quickly brings you to the PCT.

Head south on the PCT across an open scree slope below the abandoned Brown Bear Mine. The trail gently climbs to a broad shoulder offering excellent views south and southeast into Trout Creek. As you look across the valley, note the stands of snags and remnants of burnt trees, similar to those you drove through to get here. They were all damaged in the Needle Fire, which swept through

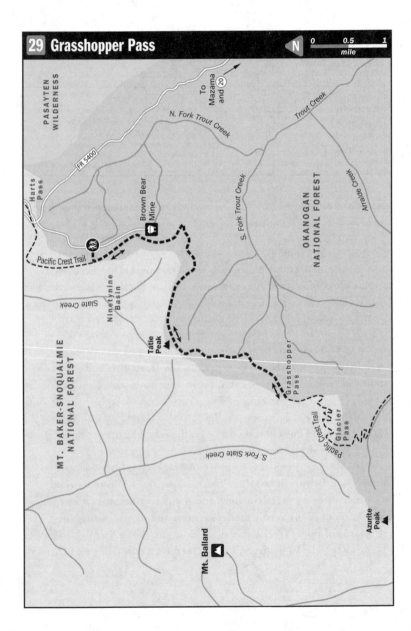

N

0   0.5   1
mile

PASAYTEN WILDERNESS

To Mazama and 20

N. Fork Trout Creek

Trout Creek

FR 5400

Harts Pass

Brown Bear Mine

S. Fork Trout Creek

OKANOGAN NATIONAL FOREST

Arralde Creek

Pacific Crest Trail

Slate Creek

Ninetynine Basin

Tatie Peak

Grasshopper Pass

Pacific Crest Trail

Glacier Pass

MT. BAKER-SNOQUALMIE NATIONAL FOREST

S. Fork Slate Creek

Mt. Ballard

Azurite Peak

FEET

7,600
7,400
7,200
7,000
6,800
6,600
6,400
6,200
6,000

1   2   3   4   5

MILES

this area back in 2003, burning thousands of acres of federal, state, and private land.

From here the trail curves to the west and follows a gentle gradient through stands of larches, mountain hemlock, and western white pines to a windswept saddle at 7,000 feet. Views open in just about every direction, with Ninetynine Basin and the Slate Peak Lookout to the north, Tatie Peak to the west, and a sea of rugged peaks to the south. If the views still aren't enough, a short, easy scramble westward will lead you to the 7,386-foot summit of Tatie Peak.

The trail travels below Tatie Peak to another saddle, from which you can see the glaciated slopes of Crater Mountain off to the northwest. From the saddle, cross the head of a feeder stream to the South Fork of Trout Creek and immediately enter a stand of larches. Descend a couple of lazy switchbacks to a long path that arrives at a forested bench, 4 miles from the trailhead. Enjoy a picnic in the shadow of Mount Ballard or spend the night at one of a few fairly protected campsites nestled among the trees (water is available from a small stream to the south).

Mt. Azurite makes a dramatic backdrop for the PCT.

To continue your journey, remain on the PCT as it heads south another mile to Grasshopper Pass (elevation 6,700 feet). Just beyond the pass, the PCT drops steeply to the broad, forested saddle of Glacier Pass. If you have extra energy, continue on a narrow path that heads south from the pass out the ridge. Ascend a knob and remain on the trail as it follows the ridgeline through scrubby trees and rocky terrain to Point 7125. Views from here are spectacular, to say the least. To the south, Golden Horn's prominent summit sits among the craggy ridgelines of the Needles and Tower Mountain. To the west is Azurite Peak's enormous east face, and beyond that lie a sea of snowcapped peaks. The 360-degree vista offers a bird's-eye view of Trout Creek and a number of named and unnamed peaks stretching out to the east. To the north you can see your entire route weave across hillsides, over saddles, and finally back to the trailhead.

DIRECTIONS   From Seattle, take I-5 north to Exit 230 and turn east on WA 20. As you head toward North Cascades National Park, note that there are limited services east of Concrete, so this is your best bet for shopping for food or getting gas. The town of Mazama is on the east side of Washington Pass, 1.5 miles past Early Winters Campground. Turn left (north) off WA 20, onto Lost River Road. Proceed to the T-intersection and turn left (west), remaining on Lost River Road. From here it's 20 miles to Harts Pass.

The road begins on pavement but soon turns into washboard gravel when it becomes FR 5400, a one-lane road with pullouts and an infamous stretch that will turn your knuckles white. Needless to say, use caution and drive slowly. As you approach Harts Pass, keep an eye out for Meadows Campground. Turn left (south) and drive 2 miles, past Meadows Campground, to the road's end.

PERMIT   Northwest Forest Pass required. Sign in at trailhead.

GPS Trailhead Coordinates	29 Grasshopper Pass
UTM Zone (WGS 84)	10U
Easting	0670912
Northing	5397860
Latitude	N48.710334°
Longitude	W120.676661°

30 Tamarack Peak

SCENERY: ✿ ✿ ✿ ✿ ✿	DISTANCE: *8–10 miles*
TRAIL CONDITION: ✿ ✿ ✿ ✿	HIKING TIME: *5–7 hours*
CHILDREN: ✿ ✿ ✿ ✿	GREEN TRAILS MAP: Pasayten Peak 18
DIFFICULTY: ✿ ✿	OUTSTANDING FEATURES: *Interesting history,*
SOLITUDE: ✿ ✿	*gorgeous alpine vistas, and brilliant colors in the fall*

Unlike many trails along the PCT, this route remains on the crest throughout the entire hike. The trail starts at 6,800 feet and travels through some of Washington's most wild high country, where rare species, including, lynx, wolves, grizzly bears, and wolverines, have been making a strong comeback. In the fall, larch trees turn a golden yellow, providing a stark contrast to the vibrant red that covers the hillsides.

🚶🚶 To begin your day exploring Pasayten Wilderness, drive 1.5 miles past the trailhead to the end of the road for a short side hike to the Slate Peak Lookout. At 7,488 feet, it is the highest lookout in the state you can drive to. Although the lookout itself is off-limits, you still get a 360-degree view of the North Cascades, and there are helpful diagrams in every corner to help you identify some of the notable peaks.

Another of the lookout's draws is its intriguing history, dating back to the mid-1900s. When the Forest Service first used this site as a fire lookout, access was via a steep, rocky trail that ran from Harts Pass to the top of the peak. In the 1950s the Cold War brought the U.S. Air Force into the region, and Slate Peak was designated the perfect spot from which to detect enemy planes. Soon a road was built, the old lookout was removed, and the top of Slate Peak was blasted off! Construction on the radar station began but, before it was finished, the project was declared obsolete. The land was given back to the Forest Service, and another fire lookout was built on top of the abandoned station. The top of the lookout now stands as tall as the original Slate Peak summit.

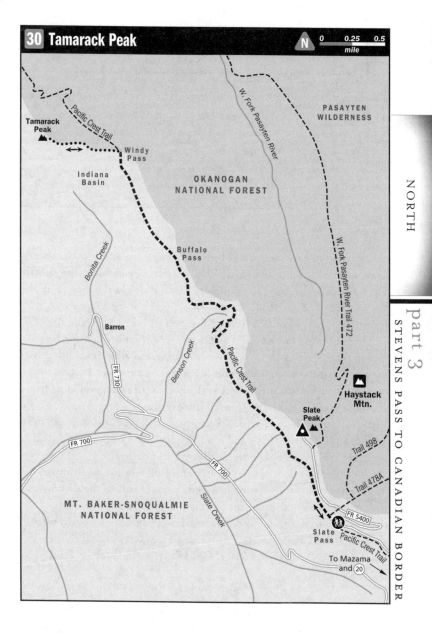

Tamarack
Peak

Pacific Crest Trail

Windy
Pass

Indiana
Basin

W. Fork Pasayten River

PASAYTEN
WILDERNESS

OKANOGAN
NATIONAL FOREST

Bonita Creek

Buffalo
Pass

W. Fork Pasayten River Trail 472

Barron

Benson Creek

Pacific Crest Trail

FR 730

FR 700

FR 700

Slate Creek

Slate
Peak

Haystack
Mtn.

Trail 498

Trail 478A

MT. BAKER-SNOQUALMIE
NATIONAL FOREST

FR 5400

Slate
Pass

Pacific Crest Trail

To Mazama
and (20)

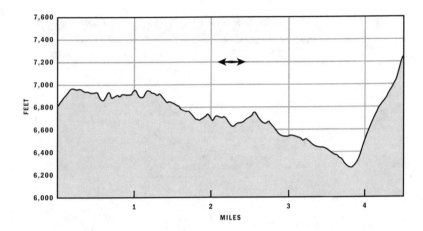

When you have had your fill of stunning views and local history here, head back down the road to the PCT trailhead (elevation 6,800 feet). From the parking lot, follow the trail north as it wraps around the west side of Slate Peak. Looking west, you can see a large scar in a hillside just below your objective, Tamarack Peak. This is the site of an old gold mine known as "The Glory Hole" that brought prospectors to the area back in 1894. Men traveled from all over and lived in the small mining town of Barron, working for a meager $2.50 per day plus meals. Most men never realized their dreams, and after two years the veins of gold disappeared underground where it was too costly to extract them. Barron became a ghost town, and over the next 40 years a few mines came and went. Today much of the land is still privately held and a few people still come to prospect.

Beyond The Glory Hole, Crater and Jack mountains shimmer in the afternoon sun; nestled between them, far off in the distance, rises Mount Baker and Mount Shuksan. Near 2 miles, the trail rounds a grassy shoulder and makes a slow descent into a basin just above Benson Creek Camp. From a small pass, views open to the north toward the Pasayten River, Gold Ridge, and Pasayten Peak.

Tamarack Peak

From here the trail bears west, contouring around an arm before resuming its northward trajectory. Along the way you pass through semiforested slopes of alpine fir and larch (also known as tamarack). In the fall, the hillsides in this area are a spectacle of vibrant colors, from the bright-yellow needles of the larches to the deep-red hues of low-lying huckleberry bushes.

Three miles from the trailhead, you arrive at Buffalo Pass (elevation 6,550 feet). Follow the PCT another mile, to the broad, sparsely forested Windy Pass (elevation 6,257 feet). For many people, especially those with kids, this is a great spot to enjoy lunch and call it a day. If you still have energy, explore cross-country to the top of Tamarack Peak, but be prepared to do some route-finding and a bit of steep traversing along the way.

From the pass, head west up a wide ridge that comes off the east side of Tamarack. Ascend through heather slopes—slick when wet!—to the ridge proper. Around 6,800 feet you enter Pasayten Wilderness, which at the time of this writing was marked by a random bright-orange sign in the middle of the slope. Game trails lead the way until the ridge narrows and you are forced to push your way through scrub trees onto the south face. When the opportunity arises (around 6,900 feet), work your way back onto the ridge, which has broadened by this point. From here it is an easy walk to the 7,290-foot summit of Tamarack Peak, where you'll most likely enjoy the panoramic views alone.

To the south lies a sea of peaks, including Silver Star, The Needles, Golden Horn, Azurite, and Ballard. Several glaciated peaks, including Mount Baker and Snowfield Peak, shine far in the distance to the west and southwest. The rain shadow effect can be seen in the dry rugged mountains that stretch to the east; to the north, the PCT stretches another 25 miles to the Canadian boarder through some of Washington's most wild and desolate country.

DIRECTIONS: FROM SEATTLE: Take I-5 north to Exit 230 and turn east on WA 20. As you head toward North Cascades National Park, note that there are limited services east of Concrete, so this is your best bet for shopping for food or getting gas. The town of Mazama is on the east side of Washington Pass, 1.5 miles east of Early Winters Campground. Turn left (north) off WA 20, onto Lost River Road. Proceed to the T-intersection and turn left (west), onto Okanogan County Road 9140. From here it is 18.5 miles to Harts Pass.

The road begins on pavement but soon turns into washboard gravel when it becomes FR 5400, a one-lane road with pullouts and an infamous stretch that will turn your knuckles white. Needless to say, use caution and drive slowly. When you arrive at Harts Pass, bear right onto the 3-mile-long Slate Peak Road (FR 5400–600). At 1.5 miles the road makes a tight switchback. Park on the small shoulder on the outside bend. There is parking for six to eight cars. If no spaces are available, there is room to park on the side of the road.

TO SLATE PEAK LOOKOUT: From the PCT trailhead, continue heading up Slate Peak Road, past another switchback and the Slate Pass Trailhead, to a permanently closed gate. It is 0.25 miles and 200 feet elevation gain to the lookout.

PERMIT: Northwest Forest Pass required. Sign in at trailhead.

GPS Trailhead Coordinates	30 Tamarack Peak
UTM Zone (WGS 84)	10U
Easting	0670913
Northing	5400310
Latitude	N48.732356°
Longitude	W120.675637°

Slate Peak Lookout (Hike 30)

Appendix A: Park Contacts

GIFFORD PINCHOT NATIONAL FOREST
www.fs.fed.us/gpnf

Forest Headquarters
10600 Northeast 51st Circle
Vancouver, WA 98682
(360) 891-5000

Columbia River Gorge National Scenic Area
902 Wasco Avenue, Suite 200
Hood River, OR 97031
(541) 308-1700

Cowlitz Valley Ranger Station
10024 US 12, P.O. Box 670
Randle, WA 98377
(360) 497-1100

Mount Adams Ranger Station
2455 Highway 141
Trout Lake, WA 98650
(509) 395-3400

LAKE CHELAN SHUTTLE SERVICE INFORMATION

Lady of the Lake
(Lake Chelan Ferry)
www.ladyofthelake.com
1418 West Woodin Avenue
Chelan, WA 98816
(509) 682-4584

Holden Shuttle
www.holdenvillage.org

Stehekin Shuttle
www.stehekin.com

MOUNT BAKER–SNOQUALMIE NATIONAL FOREST
www.fs.fed.us/r6/mbs

Forest Headquarters
2930 Wetmore Avenue, Suite 3A
Everett, WA 98201
(425) 783-6000

Enumclaw Office
450 Roosevelt Avenue East
Enumclaw, WA 98022
(360) 825-6585

North Bend Ranger Station
42404 Southeast North Bend Way
North Bend, WA 98045
(425) 888-1421

Skykomish Ranger Station
74920 Northeast Stevens Pass
   Highway
P.O. Box 305
Skykomish, WA 98288
(360) 677-2414

MOUNT RAINIER NATIONAL PARK
www.nps.gov/mora

Park Headquarters
55210 238th Avenue East
Ashford, WA 98304
(360) 569-2211

White River Wilderness Information Center
(360) 569-2211, ext. 6030

OKANOGAN–WENATCHEE NATIONAL FOREST
www.fs.fed.us/r6/wenatchee

Forest Headquarters
215 Melody Lane
Wenatchee, WA 98801
(509) 664-9200

Chelan Ranger Station
428 West Woodin Avenue
Chelan, WA 98816
(509) 682-2576

Cle Elum Ranger Station
803 West Second Street
Cle Elum, WA 98922
(509) 852-1100

Lake Wenatchee River Ranger Station
22976 WA 207
Leavenworth, WA 98826
(509) 763-3103

Leavenworth Ranger Station
600 Sherbourne Street
Leavenworth, WA 98826
(509) 548-6977

Methow Valley Ranger Station
24 West Chewuch Road
Winthrop, WA 98862
(509) 996-4003

Naches Ranger Station
10237 Highway 12
Naches, WA 98937
(509) 653-1400

NORTH CASCADES NATIONAL PARK
www.nps.gov/noca

Superintendent's Office
2105 WA 20
Sedro-Woolley, WA 98284
(360) 856-5700

Golden West Visitor Center
P.O. Box 7
Stehekin, WA 98852
(360) 856-5700, ext. 340

Marblemount Wilderness Information Center
100 Ranger Station Road
Marblemount, WA 98267
(360) 854-7245

Appendix B: Managing Agencies

SOUTH: OREGON BORDER TO WHITE PASS

1. Gillette Lake: Columbia River Gorge National Scenic Area
2. Bunker Hill: Mount Adams Ranger Station, Gifford Pinchot National Forest
3. Lemei Lake: Mount Adams Ranger Station, Gifford Pinchot National Forest
4. Horseshoe Meadow: Mount Adams Ranger Station, Gifford Pinchot National Forest
5. Nannie Ridge: Cowlitz Valley Ranger Station, Gifford Pinchot National Forest
6. Old Snowy Mountain: Naches Ranger Station, Okanogan-Wenatchee National Forest
7. Round Mountain: Cowlitz Valley Ranger Station, Gifford Pinchot National Forest

CENTRAL: WHITE PASS TO STEVENS PASS

8. Buesch and Dumbbell Lakes: Cowlitz Valley and Naches ranger stations, Gifford Pinchot National Forest
9. Laughingwater Creek: White River Wilderness Information Center, Mount Rainier National Park
10. Dewey Lake: White River Wilderness Information Center, Mount Rainier National Park and Naches Ranger District, Okanogan-Wenatchee National Forest
11. Sheep Lake and Sourdough Gap: Naches Ranger District, Okanogan-Wenatchee National Forest
12. Bullion Basin to Silver Creek: Enumclaw Office, Mount Baker-Snoqualmie National Forest
13. Big Crow Basin: Enumclaw Office, Mount Baker-Snoqualmie National Forest
14. Mirror Lake: Cle Elum Ranger Station, Okanogan-Wenatchee National Forest

15 Commonwealth Basin to Red Pass: North Bend Ranger Station, Mount Baker–Snoqualmie National Forest

16 Spectacle Lake: Cle Elum Ranger Station, Okanogan-Wenatchee National Forest

17 Cathedral and Deception Passes: Cle Elum Ranger Station, Okanogan-Wenatchee National Forest

18 Surprise and Glacier Lakes: Skykomish Ranger Station, Mount Baker–Snoqualmie National Forest

19 Hope and Mig Lakes: Skykomish Ranger Station, Mount Baker–Snoqualmie National Forest

20 Chain and Doelle Lakes: Leavenworth Ranger Station, Okanogan-Wenatchee National Forest

NORTH: STEVENS PASS TO CANADIAN BORDER

21 Lake Valhalla: Skykomish Ranger Station, Mount Baker–Snoqualmie National Forest

22 Cady Ridge to Kodak Peak: Lake Wenatchee River Ranger Station, Okanogan-Wenatchee National Forest

23 Little Giant Pass: Lake Wenatchee River Ranger Station, Okanogan-Wenatchee National Forest

24 Buck Creek Pass: Lake Wenatchee River Ranger Station, Okanogan-Wenatchee National Forest

25 Lyman Lake and Suiattle Pass: Chelan Ranger Station, Okanogan-Wenatchee National Forest

26 Agnes Creek: Golden West Visitor Center, Chelan Ranger Station, North Cascades National Park

27 Rainbow Lake and McAlester Creek: Marblemount Wilderness Information Center, North Cascades National Park and Methow Valley Ranger Station, Okanogan-Wenatchee National Forest

28 Cutthroat Pass: Methow Valley Ranger Station, North Cascades National Park

29 Grasshopper Pass: Methow Valley Ranger Station, North Cascades National Park

30 Tamarack Peak: Methow Valley Ranger Station, North Cascades National Park

Index

A

Acker Lake, 39
Adams, Don, 135
Agnes Creek, 173–179
Agnes Mountain, 175
Alpental Ski Area, 107, 109
Alpine Lakes Wilderness, 118, 125,
 130, 138
alpine vistas, best hikes for, xii
American River, 82
animal, plant, insect hazards,
 13–17
Annette Lake, 103

B

backpacks, 9
bark beetles, 157–158
Barnard Saddle, 99
Barron, 200
Basin Lake, 98
Bear Creek Mountain, 51
Bear Gap, 88
Bear Lake, 39
bears, 14–15
Benchmark Lake, 70
Big Crow Basin, 95–100
Bird Mountain, 37
biting flies, 13–14

Black Peak, 190
Blue Bell Pass, 91, 92
Bonanza Peak, 171
Bonneville Dam, 28
Bowan Mountain, 183
"Bridge of the Gods," 28
Brown Bear Mine, 193
Bryant Peak, 151
Buck Creek Pass, 161–166
Buck Mountain, 164, 165–166
Buesch and Dumbbell Lakes,
 66–72
Buffalo Pass, 201
Bullion Basin to Silver Creek,
 89–94
Bulls Tooth Ridge, 140
Bumping Lake, 77
Bunker Hill, 29–33

C

Cady Ridge to Kodak Peak,
 149–154
campfires, 9, 19
Cascade Tunnel, 144
Castle Rock, 99
Cathedral and Deception passes,
 118–124
Cave Ridge, 107

Cement Basin, 99
Chain and Doelle Lakes, 135–141
Chain Lakes, 138
Chemamus Lake, 36
Chikamin Ridge, 115, 116
children, hiking with, xii, 11
children rating, 4
Chinook Pass, 79, 81, 84
Chiwakum range, 147
Chiwawa Mountain, 171
Chiwawa River, 155, 159, 163, 164
Clark Mountain, 159
Cle Elum River, 118, 122
Clear Fork, Cowlitz River, 56
Clear Lake, 37, 38, 39, 63, 69
clothing, 7–8, 9
Cloudy Pass, 171
Columbia River Gorge, 25–26, 205
Commonwealth Basin to Red Pass, 107–111
compasses, 9
Cooper Lake, 112
Cooper River, 112
Corteo Peak, 188
Cottonwood Lake, 103
cougars, 15
Cowboy Ridge, 137
Cramer Lake, 66, 70, 71
Crater Mountain, 195, 200
Crown Point, 92
Crown Point Falls, 171

Crystal Lake, 87, 88
Crystal Mountain Ski Area, 88, 94, 95, 100
Cultus Lake, 38
Cutthroat Pass, 188–192

D

Dark Peak, 176, 184
Deception and Cathedral passes, 118–124
Deception Lake, 129
Deep Lake, 118
Deer Lake, 39, 68
Delate Falls, 115
Dewey Lake, 79–83
difficult hikes, xiii
difficulty rating, 4
Dishpan Gap, 153
distance rating, 4
Doelle and Chain Lakes, 135–141
Dog Lake, 61–62, 71
dogs, best hikes with, xii
Douglas, William O., 79
Douglas fir, 31
drinking water, 6–7
Dry Lake Camp, 44
Dumbbell Lake, 66–72
Dumbell Mountain, 169

E

easy hikes, xiii
elevation profiles, 1–2

Elk Lake, 39
Elk Pass, 56
emergencies
    animal, plant, insect hazards,
        13–17
    first-aid kits, 9, 10–11
    general safety, 11–13
equipment, hiking, 8–10

F

features, trips, 4
fires, 9, 19
first-aid kits, 9, 10–11
flies, biting, 13–14
food, 12
footwear, 8
forest management practices, 31,
    33
Fortress Mountain, 164
Frisco Mountain, 180
Frosty Pass, 140

G

garbage disposal, 19
giardia parasite, 6–7
Gifford Pinchot National Forest
        contacts, 205
Gillette Lake, 24–28
Ginnette Lake, 60, 63
Glacier and Surprise Lakes,
        125–129
Glacier Lake, 116, 129

Glacier Pass, 197
Glacier Peak, 151, 159, 165
Glacier Peak Wilderness, 161, 163,
        169, 175
Glory Hole, The, 200
Goat Lake, 57, 97, 99
Goats Rocks Wilderness, 46, 48,
        51, 56, 60, 61
Golden Horn, 197, 202
GPS trailhead coordinates, 2–3
GPS units, 1
Granite Pass, 190
Grasshopper Pass, 193–197
Great Northern Railroad (GNR),
        144
guidebook, how to use this, 1–4
Gunsight Peak, 175
Guye Peak, 107

H

Hart Lake, 167, 170, 171
Harts Pass, 193, 203
Helmet Butte, 165
Hen Skin Lake, 92
High Pass, 164
hikes. *See also specific hike*
    Central: White Pass to Stevens
        Pass, 64–141
    GPS trailhead coordinates, 2–3
    managing agencies, 207–208
    North: Stevens Pass to
        Canadian border, 142–204

hikes *(continued)*
    park contacts, 205–206
    profiles, 3
    recommendations by type,
        xii–xiii
    South: Oregon border to White
        Pass, 22–63
    star rating system, 3–4
hiking
    backcountry advice, 18–19
    equipment, 8–10
    with kids, 11
    ten essentials, 9–10
    trail etiquette, 20
hiking time, 4
Hinch, Steve, 3
Hogsback Ridge, 61
Holden, James Henry, 167
Holden Lake, 169
Holden Village, 167, 169, 173,
        176, 179, 205
Hope and Mig Lakes, 130–134
Horseshoe Meadow, 41–45
Hyas Lake, 118, 120, 121, 123, 124
hypothermia, 13

I

Indian Heaven Wilderness,
        34–35, 37
insect, animal, plant hazards,
        13–17, 157–158

J

Jack Mountain, 200
Jim Town, 93
Josephine Lake, 139
Junction Lake, 39

K

Kachess Lake, 112
Keechelus Lake, 101
Kehr, Bruce, 135
kids
    best overnight hikes with, xii
    hiking with, 11
knives, 9
Kodak Peak, 153

L

Lake Chelan, 167, 173
Lake Chelan National Recreation
        Area, 183
Lake Chelan Shuttle, 205
Lake Keechelus, 111
Lake Sally Ann, 152
Lake Valhalla, 144–148
Lakeview Mountain, 49
land access regulations, 19
Laughingwater Creek, 73–78
Leech Lake, 58
Lemah Range, 114
Lemei Lake, 34–40
Liberty Cap, 165

Lichtenberg Mountain, 144, 146, 147
lights, 9
Little Giant Pass, 155–160
Long John Lake, 70
Longfellow Mountain, 151
Looking Glass Lake, 44
loop hikes, best, xii
Lundin Peak, 111
Lutz Lake, 53–54
Lyman Lake and Suiattle Pass, 167–172

M

managing agencies, 207–208
maps 9. *See also specific hike*
  Oregon border to White Pass, 22
  overview, key, 1
  Stevens Pass to Canadian border, 142
  White Pass to Stevens Pass, 64
McAlester Creek and Rainbow Lake, 180–187
McAlester Lake, 186
McAlester Mountain, 186
McAlester Pass, 185
McCall Basin, 54, 55
McGregor Mountain, 173, 182, 183, 184
Michael Lake, 118

midges (no-see-ums), 14
Mig Lake, 20–21, 130–134
Miners Lake, 92
Mirror Lake, 101–106
Monte Cristo, 153
mosquitoes, 13–14
Mount Adams, 41, 43, 44, 48, 63, 77, 86, 205
Mount Baker, 200, 202
Mount Baker-Snoqualmie National Forest contacts, 205
Mount Ballard, 195
Mount Daniel, 120, 123, 129
Mount Goode, 182
Mount Rainier, 44, 55, 63, 76, 77, 91
Mount Rainier National Park, 41, 73, 78, 79, 83, 87, 88, 205
Mount Shuksan, 200
Mount St. Helens, 37, 38, 77
Mount St. Helens National Volcanic Monument, 41
Mt. Azurite, 195, 197, 202
Mt. Thompson, 110
Munger, Thorton T., 31
mushrooms, poisonous, 16

N

Naches Peak, 79
Nannie Peak, 46, 48
Nannie Ridge, 46–50

Napeequa River, 159
Needle Fire, 193, 195
Needle Peak, 179
Needles, The, 202
Norse Peak, 92, 97
North Cascades National Park,
    187, 197, 203, 206
North Fork Tieton, 51
Northwest Forest Pass, 19

O

Okanogan-Wenatchee National
    Forest contacts, 206
Old Snowy Mountain, 51–57
One Lake, 78
Outdoor Navigation with GPS (Hinch),
    3
outstanding features, 4
overview map and key, 1

P

parasites, waterborne, 6–7
park contacts, 205–206
Pasayten Wilderness, 191, 198
pass, Northwest Forest, 19
PCT (Pacific Crest Trail)
    best hikes on, xiii
    hikes central: White Pass to
        Stevens Pass, 64–141
    hikes north: Stevens Pass to
        Canadian border, 142–204
    hikes south: Oregon border to

    White Pass, 22–63
    tips for enjoying, 17–18
    weather, seasons, 4–6
permits, Northwest Forest Pass,
    19
Pete Lake, 112, 114, 116
Pickhandle Gap, 92
Pieper Pass, 129
pine bark beetles, 157–158
Placid Lake, 34, 36
plant, animal, insect hazards,
    13–17, 157–158
Plummer Mountain, 178
Poe Mountain, 154
poisonous plants, 16–17
Prieb, Wes, 167, 169
profiles, elevation and hike, 1, 3
purifying water, 6–7

R

Rainbow Lake and McAlester
    Creek, 180–187
Rainbow Pass, 184
rating system for hikes, 3–4
rattlesnakes, 15–16
recommended hikes, by type,
    xii–xiii
Red Mountain, 109, 163
Red Pass, Commonwealth Basin
    to, 107–111
Rimrock Lake, 63
Robin Lake, 122

Rooster Comb, 138
Roslyn, 117, 124
Round Mountain, 58–63

S

safety
  animal, plant, insect hazards,
    13–17
  first-aid kits, 9, 10–11
  general, 11–13
Salmon La Sac, 124
Sand Lake, 69
Sandalee Glacier, 182
Sawtooth Huckleberry Fields, 34
scenery rating, 4
Scout Pass, 92
seasons, weather, 4–6
Seymour Peak, 81
Sheep Lake, 44, 48, 49, 84–88
shelter, 10
Silver Peak, 101
Silver Star, 190
Sitting Bull, 176, 177
Skykomish, 122
Skykomish River, 153
Skyline Ridge, 144
Slate Peak Lookout, 195, 198, 204
snakes, hazardous, 15–16
Snoqualmie Mountain, 109
Snoqualmie Pass, 111
Snoqualmie Ski Area, 111
Snowfield Peak, 202

solitude
  best hikes for, xiii
  rating, 4
Sourdough Gap, 84–88
Spark Plug Lake, 129
Spark Plug Mountain, 127
Spectacle Lake, 112–117
Spiral Butte, 61–62, 69, 71
Squaw Lake, 118
star rating system for hikes, 3–4
Stehekin, 172, 173, 179
Stehekin Shuttle, 205
Stevens Pass, 134–137, 141, 142,
  144, 148, 160
Stiletto Peak, 180
streams, crossing, 12
Suiattle Pass and Lyman Lake,
  167–172
summits, best hikes to, xii
sun protection, 9
Surprise and Glacier Lakes,
  125–129
Surprise Mountain, 129
Susan Jane Lake, 138–139
swimming holes, best hikes for, xii

T

Table Mountain, 4, 26–28
Tamarack Peak, 198–204
Tatie Peak, 195
temperature, weather, 4–6, 18
Three Lakes, 73, 75

INDEX

Three Queens Mountain, 115
Tieton Pass, 53
Tieton Peak, 55
times, hiking, 4
Tinkham Peak, 103, 105
Tipsoo Lake, 83
Topo USA, 1
Tower Mountain, 190, 197
trail condition rating, 4
trail etiquette, 20
trail maps 1. *See also specific hike*
trails, staying on designated, 12
Trap Lake, 134
Trinity, 163
Trout Lake, 40
Tuck Lake, 122
Tucquala Lake, 124
Tunnel Creek, 130, 132
Tupshin Peak, 184
Twin Lakes, 101, 103, 104
Twin Peaks, 60
Twisp Pass, 186
Two Lakes, 77

U

Upper Hyas Lake, 121, 123, 124
UTM coordinates, 2–3

W

Walupt Creek, 50
Walupt Creek Campground, 46
Walupt Lake, 49
Waptus Lake, 112, 118
Wards Pass, 153
waste disposal, 19
water, drinking, 6–7, 9, 12
weather, seasons, 4–6, 18
Wenatchee Ridge, 151, 154
West Nile virus, 14
White Goat Mountain, 184
White Mountains, 166
White Pass, 57, 58
White Salmon River, 43
wildflowers
    best hikes for viewing, xii
    picking, 20
wildlife, viewing, 20
William O. Douglas Wilderness,
    68, 71, 76–77, 79, 92
Wind River area, 31
Windy Pass, 202

Y

Yakama Indian Nation, 34

About the Author

ADRIENNE SCHAEFER'S LOVE OF NATURE and outdoor pursuits began at a young age, building forts and camping out with her family in the foot-hills of Washington's North Cascades. As she got older, her love turned into a lifestyle, and she decided to pursue a career in the outdoor industry.

A bachelor's degree in outdoor recreation led her to a variety of outdoor-based jobs, including working for the National Park Service and U.S Forest Service as a trail crew member, wildland firefighter, and a climbing ranger on Mt. Rainier. She spends winters on the slopes of Stevens Pass as a professional ski patroller, and summers guiding for Anew Outdoors. Her most recent endeavor is ActiveGirl Escapes, a group of women in her hometown of Leavenworth, Washington, who came together to offer year-round outdoor activities.

When Adrienne's not working, she roams the high country of the North Cascades or spends time at home, where she enjoys trail running, gardening, and hanging out with her husband, John, and their dog, Lemah.